new interchange

Dorothy E. Zemach

video activity book

3

CAMBRIDGE
UNIVERSITY PRESS

PUBLISHED BY THE PRESS SYNDICATE OF THE UNIVERSITY OF CAMBRIDGE
The Pitt Building, Trumpington Street, Cambridge, United Kingdom

CAMBRIDGE UNIVERSITY PRESS
The Edinburgh Building, Cambridge CB2 2RU, UK
40 West 20th Street, New York, NY 10011-4211, USA
477 Williamstown Road, Port Melbourne, VIC 3207, Australia
Ruiz de Alarcón 13, 28014 Madrid, Spain
Dock House, The Waterfront, Cape Town 8001, South Africa

http://www.cambridge.org

The publisher has used its best endeavors to ensure that the URLs for Web sites referred
to in this book are correct and active at the time of going to press. However, the publisher
has no responsibility for the Web sites and can make no guarantee that a site will remain
live or that the content is or will remain appropriate.

Printed in Hong Kong, China

Typeface New Century Schoolbook   *System* QuarkXPress®   [AH]

A catalog record for this book is available from the British Library

ISBN 0 521 62844 X Student's Book 3
ISBN 0 521 62843 1 Student's Book 3A
ISBN 0 521 62842 3 Student's Book 3B
ISBN 0 521 62841 5 Workbook 3
ISBN 0 521 62840 7 Workbook 3A
ISBN 0 521 62839 3 Workbook 3B
ISBN 0 521 62838 5 Teacher's Edition 3
ISBN 0 521 62837 7 Teacher's Manual
ISBN 0 521 62836 9 Class Audio Cassettes 3
ISBN 0 521 62834 2 Student's Audio Cassette 3A
ISBN 0 521 62832 6 Student's Audio Cassette 3B
ISBN 0 521 62835 0 Class Audio CDs 3
ISBN 0 521 62833 4 Student's Audio CD 3A
ISBN 0 521 62831 8 Student's Audio CD 3B
ISBN 0 521 95019 8 Audio Sampler 1–3

Also available
ISBN 0 521 01094 2 Video 3 (NTSC)
ISBN 0 521 01100 0 Video 3 (PAL)
ISBN 0 521 01097 7 Video 3 (SECAM)
ISBN 0 521 01091 8 Video Activity Book 3
ISBN 0 521 01088 8 Video Teacher's Guide 3
ISBN 0 521 89206 6 Video Sampler 3
ISBN 0 521 62882 2 Placement Test
ISBN 0 521 77377 6 Lab Guide 3
ISBN 0 521 77376 8 Lab Cassettes 3
ISBN 0 521 80575 9 Teacher-Training Video
                  with Video Manual
Forthcoming
ISBN 0 521 62882 2 *New Interchange / Passages*
                  Placement and Evaluation Package

Art direction, book design, and layout services: Adventure House, NYC
Illustrators: Adventure House, Keith Bendis, David Coulson, Felipe Galindo,
          Daniel Vasconcellos, S.B. Whitehead

Plan of Video Activity Book 3

1 p2 **Dream Date** A young woman chooses one of three men for her date on a dating game show.
Functional Focus Expressing feelings; describing personalities
Grammar Clauses containing *it* with adverbial clauses
Vocabulary Personality types

2 Documentary p6 **Urban artist** A muralist talks about his career and what motivates his painting.
Functional Focus Describing a job
Grammar Gerunds as subjects and objects
Vocabulary Words to describe art

3 p10 **Kid sister** A woman asks her friend to look after her younger sister overnight.
Functional Focus Asking favors
Grammar Indirect requests
Vocabulary Requests and responses

4 p14 **Bigfoot lives!** Three friends go on a camping trip and one plays a practical joke.
Functional Focus Telling a story in the past
Grammar Past tense verbs – past continuous, simple past, and past perfect
Vocabulary Descriptions

5 Documentary p18 **Travel World** Reporters around the world ask people about cross-cultural experiences.
Functional Focus Describing customs
Grammar Expectations – (not) expected to, (not) supposed to, (not) customary to, (not) acceptable to
Vocabulary Travel abroad

6 p22 **Heartbreak Hotel** A couple's hope for a relaxing weekend at a quaint hotel is dashed.
Functional Focus Describing problems; making complaints
Grammar *Need* with passive infinitives and gerunds
Vocabulary Words to describe problems

7 Documentary p26 **Saving Florida's manatees** Experts discuss conservation efforts to save Florida's manatees.
Functional Focus Describing environmental problems and solutions
Grammar The passive and prepositions of cause
Vocabulary The environment

8 Documentary p30 **Salsa!** People all over the world are learning how to dance salsa.
Functional Focus Talking about learning methods
Grammar Gerunds and infinitives
Vocabulary Words related to learning

9 p34 **Stress relief** A woman seeks advice from a co-worker on how to relieve stress.
Functional Focus Making suggestions
Grammar Gerunds, infinitives, base-form verbs, and negative questions
Vocabulary Idioms related to stress

10 Documentary p38 **Fort Steele Heritage Town** Visitors to Fort Steele in Canada get transported back in time.
Functional Focus Talking about the past
Grammar Referring to time in the past with adverbs and prepositions
Vocabulary Words to describe life long ago

11 p42 **If only . . .** Five college friends get together to talk about their past, present, and future.
Functional Focus Describing regrets about the past
Grammar Time clauses with *should have* + past participle and *if* clauses + past perfect
Vocabulary Words to describe behavior

12 Documentary p46 **Need information? AskJeeves.com** The success of an Internet search engine company is discussed.
Functional Focus Discussing what makes a business successful
Grammar Infinitive clauses and phrases of purpose
Vocabulary The Internet

13 p50 **Car trouble** A groom and his best man get delayed on the way to the wedding.
Functional Focus Offering opinions and advice
Grammar Past modals
Vocabulary Words to describe car trouble

14 Documentary p54 **Behind the scenes in TV news** A look at how TV news is produced
Functional Focus Describing how something is made
Grammar The passive to describe process
Vocabulary The language of TV news production

15 Documentary p58 **Entertainment or environment? A town debates.** The building of an amphitheater stirs controversy among citizens.
Functional Focus Talking about town rules
Grammar Passive modals
Vocabulary Describing locations

16 Documentary p62 **The ultimate challenge** Four women cross Antarctica without the help of dogs, machines, or men.
Functional Focus Talking about challenges
Grammar Complex noun phrases with gerunds
Vocabulary Words related to an expedition

Introduction

NEW INTERCHANGE

New Interchange is a revision of *Interchange,* one of the world's most successful and popular English courses. *New Interchange* is a multi-level course in English as a second or foreign language for young adults and adults. The course covers the four skills of listening, speaking, reading, and writing, as well as improving pronunciation and building vocabulary. Particular emphasis is placed on listening and speaking. The primary goal of the course is to teach communicative competence, that is, the ability to communicate in English according to the situation, purpose, and roles of the participants. The language used in *New Interchange* is American English; however, the course reflects the fact that English is the major language of international communication and is not limited to any one country, region, or culture. Level Three takes students from the intermediate level up to the high-intermediate level.

Level Three builds on the foundations for accurate and fluent communication already established in Level Two by extending grammatical, lexical, and functional skills. The syllabus covered in Level Three also incorporates a review of some key language from Level Two, allowing Student's Book 3 to be used with students who have not studied with previous levels.

THE VIDEO COURSE

New Interchange Video 3 is designed to complement the Student's Book or to be used independently as the basis for a short listening and speaking course.

As a complement to the Student's Book, the Video provides a variety of entertaining and instructive live-action sequences. Each video sequence provides further practice related to the topics, language, and vocabulary introduced in the corresponding unit of the Student's Book.

As the basis for a short, free-standing course, the Video serves as an exciting vehicle for introducing and practicing useful conversational language used in everyday situations.

The Video Activity Book contains a wealth of activities that reinforce and extend the content of the Video, whether it is used to supplement the Student's Book or as the basis for an independent course. The Video Teacher's Guide provides thorough support for both situations.

COURSE LENGTH

The Video contains a mix of entertaining, dramatized sequences and authentic documentaries for a total of sixteen sequences. These vary slightly in length, but in general, the sequences are approximately five to eleven minutes each.

The accompanying units in the Video Activity Book are designed for maximum flexibility and provide anywhere from 45 to 90 minutes of classroom activity. Optional activities described in the Video Teacher's Guide may be used to extend the lesson as needed.

MORE ABOUT THE COURSE COMPONENTS

Video

The sixteen video sequences complement Units 1 through 16 of *New Interchange* Student's Book 3. There are seven dramatized sequences and nine documentary sequences. Although linked to the topic of the corresponding Student's Book unit, each dramatized sequence presents a new situation and introduces characters who do not appear in the text. Each documentary sequence is based on authentic, unscripted interviews with people in various situations, and serves to illustrate how language is used by real people in real situations. This element of diversity helps keep students' interest high and also allows the Video to be used effectively as a free-standing course. At the same time, the language used in the video sequences reflects the structures and vocabulary of the Student's Book, which is based on an integrated syllabus that links grammar and communicative functions.

Video Activity Book

The Video Activity Book contains sixteen units that correspond to the video sequences, and is designed to facilitate the effective use of the Video in the classroom. Each unit includes previewing, viewing, and postviewing activities that provide learners with step-by-step support and guidance in understanding and working with the events and language of the sequence. Learners expand their cultural awareness, develop skills and strategies for communicating effectively, and use language creatively.

Video Teacher's Guide

The Video Teacher's Guide contains detailed suggestions for how to use the Video and the Video Activity Book in the classroom, and includes an overview of video teaching techniques, unit-by-unit notes, and a range of optional extension activities. The Video Teacher's Guide also includes answers to the activities in the Video Activity Book and photocopiable transcripts of the video sequences.

VIDEO IN THE CLASSROOM

The use of video in the classroom can be an exciting and effective way to teach and learn. As a medium, video both motivates and entertains students. The *New Interchange* Video is a unique resource that does the following:

- Depicts dynamic, natural contexts for language use.

- Presents authentic language as well as cultural information about speakers of English through engaging story lines.

- Enables learners to use visual information to enhance comprehension.

- Focuses on the important cultural dimension of learning a language by actually showing how speakers of the language live and behave.

- Allows learners to observe the gestures, facial expressions, and other aspects of body language that accompany speech.

WHAT EACH UNIT OF THE VIDEO ACTIVITY BOOK CONTAINS

Each unit of the Video Activity Book is divided into four sections: *Preview*, *Watch the Video*, *Follow-up*, and *Language Close-up*. In general, these four sections include, but are not limited to, the following types of activities:

Preview

Culture The culture previews introduce the topics of the video sequences and provide important background and cultural information. They can be presented in class as reading and discussion activities, or students can read and complete them as homework.

Vocabulary The vocabulary activities introduce and practice the essential vocabulary of the video sequences through a variety of interesting tasks.

Guess the Story/Guess the Facts The Guess the Story (or in some units Guess the Facts) activities allow students to make predictions about characters and their actions by watching the video sequences without the sound or by looking at photos in the Video Activity Book. These schema-building activities help to improve students' comprehension when they watch the sequences with the sound.

Watch the Video

Get the Picture These initial viewing activities help students gain global understanding of the sequences by focusing on gist. Activity types vary from unit to unit, but typically involve watching for key information needed to complete a chart, answer questions, or put events in order.

Watch for Details In these activities, students focus on more detailed meaning by watching and listening for specific information to complete tasks about the story line and the characters or the information in the documentaries.

What's Your Opinion? In these activities, students respond to the sequences by making inferences about the characters' actions, feelings, and motivations, and by stating their opinions about issues and topics.

Follow-up

Role Play, Interview, and Other Expansion Activities This section includes communicative activities based on the sequences in which students extend and personalize what they have learned.

Language Close-up

What Did They Say? These cloze activities focus on the specific language in the sequences by having students watch and listen in order to fill in missing words in conversations.

Grammar and Functional Activities In these activities, which are titled to reflect the structural and functional focus of a particular unit, students practice, in a meaningful way, the grammatical structures and functions presented in the video sequences.

Dream Date

1 CULTURE

In North America most people start dating in their teens and early twenties. They meet at school or work, or are introduced by friends. On dates, they go out in couples or in groups to movies, sporting events, and meals. Traditionally, the man paid for the date, but modern couples may decide to split the bill or let the person who made the invitation pay for both people.

How do people in your country meet each other? What do friends or dating couples like to do together? Where are some popular places to go? When a man and a woman (or a group of friends) go out together, who pays?

2 VOCABULARY *Personality types*

Pair work How would you describe the people below? Choose a description from the box.

a good conversationalist	easygoing	generous
ambitious	✔egotistical	straightforward

1) Jill is always talking about herself. She thinks she's better than other people.
   A: I think she's *egotistical*.
   B: Yes, I agree.

2) Mike is very relaxed. Nothing seems to upset him.

3) Paul always tells people exactly what he thinks. He doesn't hide his feelings.

4) Erika has big plans and works hard to achieve them.

5) John asks a lot of questions, and he's interested in what I have to say.

6) Leah is a great friend. She's giving of her time and energy, and she also forgives others easily.

3 GUESS THE STORY

Sarah is going to choose one of these men to be her date. How do you think she will decide? Who will she choose?

Bachelor 1   Bachelor 2   Bachelor 3

 **Watch the video**

4 GET THE PICTURE

A Look at your answers to Exercise 3. Did you guess correctly?

B Check (✔) the things Sarah asked the bachelors. Then compare with a partner.

☐ What's your idea of the perfect date?
☐ How old are you?
☐ What's your favorite sport?
☐ Tell me something positive and something negative about yourself.
☐ Finish this sentence: "I think it's disgusting when . . ."
☐ Finish this sentence: "My ideal date has . . ."

C What words describe Sarah and the bachelors? Write the correct word under each picture. Then compare with a partner.

easygoing	egotistical	excited	straightforward

5 WATCH FOR DETAILS

Correct the mistakes below. Then compare with a partner.

> twenty-nine
> Bachelor 1 is ~~thirty-nine~~ years old. He's a former college football coach
> from Pocatello, Idaho, who loves playing or watching almost every kind of
> game. Bachelor 2 is a thirty-year-old doctor from Los Angeles. Everyone
> should know his soap opera, *Our World*. Bachelor 3 comes from Sarah's
> hometown of Ames, Iowa. In his free time, he enjoys swimming and surfing
> the Internet. He and Sarah went to college together.

6 *WHO SAID WHAT?*

Who said the sentences below? Check (✔) the correct answers. Then compare with a partner.

	Bachelor 1	Bachelor 2	Bachelor 3
1) I'd be too embarrassed to tell you the truth.	☐	☐	☐
2) It really bothers me when people lie.	☐	☐	☐
3) I would take you to my favorite nightclub where everybody knows me.	☐	☐	☐
4) I'd take you out to a nice dinner.	☐	☐	☐
5) I think I'm a pretty good friend, and people trust me.	☐	☐	☐
6) Actually, I'm pretty good at most things I do.	☐	☐	☐
7) Well, I guess I'm pretty easygoing.	☐	☐	☐

Follow-up

7 *ROLE PLAY* *Let's play* Dream Date*!*

A *Pair work* Imagine you are Sarah. Add two more questions to ask the bachelors.

1) What's your idea of the ideal date?

2) Tell me two things about yourself: one positive and one negative.

3) Finish this sentence: "I can't stand it when . . ."

4) ....

5) ....

B *Group work* Now join another pair. Three of you are bachelors. The fourth person is Sarah.

Sarah: Take turns asking the three bachelors your questions. Then choose your dream date.

Bachelors: Answer Sarah's questions.
Try to get Sarah to choose you as her dream date.

Language close-up

8 WHAT DID THEY SAY?

Watch the video and complete the conversations. Then practice them.

Sarah is asking the bachelors to complete a few sentences.

Sarah: OK. Uh, Bachelor Number 1, finish this sentence:
"I .... it when . . ."

Bachelor 1: I .... it when people are ....
while I'm .... the football game on TV.

Sarah: OK. Uh, Bachelor Number 3, finish this sentence:
"I .... it's .... when . . ."

Bachelor 3: I .... it's .... when
I'm at an expensive .... and I don't get
the .... I deserve.

Sarah: OK. Bachelor Number 2: "It ....
me when . . ."

Bachelor 2: It .... me when people get .... and they get
into .... over unimportant things. I just
think people should be more .... and treat
each other ....

9 CLAUSES CONTAINING IT WITH ADVERBIAL CLAUSES
Expressing feelings

A Complete the sentences about dates or friendships with phrases from the box. Then add two more statements of your own.

1) I can't stand it *when my date arrives late* .

2) It makes me happy... .

3) I like it ....

4) It bothers me ....

5) It really upsets me ....

6) It embarrasses me ....

7) ....

8) ....

B *Pair work* Compare your statements with a partner. Which of your partner's statements are true for you?

> ✔ arrive late
> forget to call me
> lie to me
> make me feel special
> send me flowers
> talk during a movie

2 Urban artist

1 CULTURE

Public art appears in many forms in many places. Airports, hospitals, government buildings, libraries, schools, and parks feature different types of art such as paintings, murals, sculpture, tapestries, statues, fountains – even carpets. Public art may bring a sense of pride or show the spirit of the community, honor local artists, educate or inspire visitors, or just beautify a place. The next time you visit a public place, be sure to keep an eye out for the art around you!

Talk about the public art in your community or the place where you live now. What kinds are there? Where are they located? What kinds of art do you like? Describe some of your favorite artworks.

2 VOCABULARY *Art*

A What words do you think describe these works of art? Use words from the box. (Words can be used more than once.) Can you add more words?

| colorful | creative | dull | exciting | political | spiritual |

 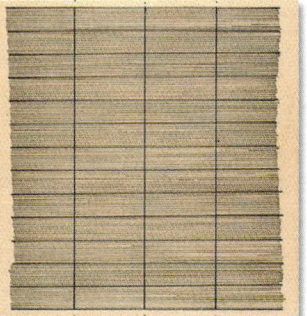  

....
....
....

B *Pair work* Share your opinions with a partner. Have conversations like this:

A: In my opinion, the first picture is dull.
B: I agree. It's not very exciting. **or** Really? I think it's very creative!

6

3 GUESS THE FACTS

***Watch the first minute and a half
of the video with the sound off.***
What kind of art do you think José creates?

 **Watch the video**

4 GET THE PICTURE

A What are the steps in creating a mural? Number the steps (1 to 6).
Then compare with a partner.

.... buy materials   .... plan and draw ideas

.... find funding   .... set a schedule for the workers

.... paint the mural   ....*1*.... look for a wall

B *Pair work* Take turns talking about which steps you would or would not enjoy doing.

5 WATCH FOR DETAILS

A Check (✔) **True** or **False**. Then correct the false statements. Compare
with a partner.

	True	*False*	
1) José Curbelo works in inner cities.	☐	☐	....
2) Public art is a recent trend.	☐	☐	....
3) José has been interested in art since he was a child.	☐	☐	....
4) After high school, he started his own business.	☐	☐	....
5) He has never been to art school.	☐	☐	....
6) The business owner always pays for the mural.	☐	☐	....
7) José's workers are older than he is.	☐	☐	....
8) José works in California now.	☐	☐	....

B *Pair work* Now write two of your own statements. Have your partner
tell you if they are true or false.

....

....

6 WHAT'S YOUR OPINION?

A What does José Curbelo prefer in a work situation? Check (✔) the phrases that describe what he prefers. Then compare with a partner.

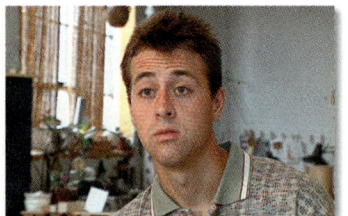

1) ☐ working alone	☐ working with people
2) ☐ making a lot of money	☐ doing interesting work
3) ☐ following a routine	☐ doing something different every day
4) ☐ working outside	☐ working in an office
5) ☐ being the boss	☐ having a boss

B *Pair work* Which of the situations in part A would you prefer?
Ask and answer questions like this:

A: Would you prefer working alone or working with people?
B: I'd prefer working alone. How about you?

C *Pair work* Which of the jobs below match the descriptions in part A?

accountant	doctor	flight attendant	marine biologist	songwriter
architect	executive	journalist	model	teacher

Make sentences like this:

A: An *accountant* would probably prefer *working alone*.
B: I agree. And a *doctor* would probably prefer *working with people*.

Follow-up

7 BEAUTIFYING YOUR AREA

A *Pair work* Think about the town or city where you are now. Which public places could you make more beautiful? How would you do this? Complete the chart.

Public places	Things to do
the neighborhood park	put a fountain there; plant flowers

B *Group work* Now join another pair. Choose two or three suggestions and tell them your ideas. Make comparisons like this:

A: Let's put a fountain in front of the library. Listening to water is very relaxing.
B: Yes, but a sculpture isn't as expensive as a fountain.
C: That's true, but I think a sculpture is less exciting than a fountain.

Language close-up

8 WHAT DID HE SAY?

Watch the video and complete the commentary. Then compare with a partner.

José Curbelo explains why he enjoys painting murals.

I love .... with .... I love .... my
own thing, I love .... my own paycheck, and I like
to be .... in the life of the . . . .
.... on murals, you're at one .... – at one
street corner – for twelve, fourteen .... a day, and you
see .... that goes on.
In my .... , the murals are .... to
the life of a community, ... ever since way back
when – .... of thousands of years ago – people
have .... themselves in a .... way.
Whether for .... reasons or for ....
reasons, or just to be .... , people have expressed
themselves on .... , and I wouldn't be .... what I'm
doing now if . . . you know, ... didn't write on .... you know,
thousands of years ago or write on .... trains in the seventies.

9 GERUNDS AS SUBJECTS AND OBJECTS Describing a job

A Complete the sentences about a job using the gerund forms of the words and
phrases in the box. Then guess the job described.

| encourage | organize the game schedule | work on weekends |
| improve their skills | stay in shape | ✔ work with children |

1) I enjoy ....*working with children*.... ; it helps me feel young.

2) .... is easy with all the running around I have to do!

3) I don't always enjoy .... ,
   but that's when our games are held.

4) At the end of the season, we have a big tournament, so I spend a lot of time
   ....

5) I help players concentrate on ....

6) .... weaker players helps the whole team improve.

Job described: ....

B *Pair work* Choose a job and describe your duties. Can your partner guess your job?

3 Kid sister

Preview

1 CULTURE

Read this advice to baby-sitters in the United States.

- Ask the parents to show you the location of emergency exits, smoke detectors, and fire extinguishers.
- Make sure you have the telephone number of where the parents are going.
- If the children are up, know their location at all times and never leave them alone too long. If the children are asleep, check on them about every fifteen minutes.
- Always get approval if you would like to have a visitor.
- In an emergency: Call 911. Identify yourself by name, say you are baby-sitting, and state the problem. Say where you are and give the phone number you are calling from.

Is baby-sitting popular in your country? What would you enjoy about baby-sitting? What would be challenging? Write some suggestions or rules for baby-sitters to add to the list above.

2 VOCABULARY Requests and responses

Pair work Match each request with a response. Then practice the requests and responses.

..*d*.. 1) Is it all right if I use your phone?

.... 2) Would you mind my using your car?

.... 3) Is it OK if I drop her off?

.... 4) Could you ask her to bring something?

.... 5) I was wondering if you could help me out.

.... 6) Would you mind if she stayed with you?

a) No, go ahead. The keys are on the table.

b) OK. I'll tell her.

c) Sure. What can I do?

d) No, sorry. I'm expecting a call.

e) Not at all. I'd be happy to have her.

f) Sure. Or I can pick her up.

3 GUESS THE STORY

Watch the first two minutes of the video with the sound off.
What do you think the women are talking about on the phone?

 **Watch the video**

4 GET THE PICTURE

First put the pictures in order (1 to 6). Then write the correct request
under each picture. Compare with a partner.

Would you turn the volume down?
Is it all right if I take a shower?
Is it all right if I use your phone
   to call one of my friends?

Is it OK if I drop her off on my way to the airport?
Would you mind my using it?
Would you mind if I listened to some of them?

....

....

....

....

....

....

....

....

....

....

....

....

5 MAKING INFERENCES

Which statements are probably true? Which are probably false?
Check (✔) your answers. Then compare with a partner.

	True	False
1) Abby is in a hurry.	☐	☐
2) Abby and Kathy live together.	☐	☐
3) Renee thinks it will be easy to get along with Kathy.	☐	☐
4) Kathy likes pizza a lot.	☐	☐
5) Kathy talks to Abby on the phone.	☐	☐
6) Kathy is a tidy person.	☐	☐
7) Abby is surprised that Kathy and Renee became friends.	☐	☐

6 WHO SAID WHAT?

Who said the sentences below? Check (✔) the correct answers. Then compare with a partner.

	Abby	Renee	Kathy
1) She's going through a stage.	☐	☐	☐
2) Wow, you've got a lot of CDs!	☐	☐	☐
3) Is there anything I can get for you?	☐	☐	☐
4) Do you have anything to eat around here?	☐	☐	☐
5) You were reading *Harry Potter*?	☐	☐	☐
6) Actually, I'm late.	☐	☐	☐

Follow-up

7 ROLE PLAY *Can you help me out?*

A *Pair work*

Student A: You're planning a big party for this weekend. You want your friend (Student B) to help you. Write your requests in the box below. Then ask your friend for help.

Student B: Accept or decline your friend's (Student A's) requests.

1)	*I was wondering if I could borrow your vacuum cleaner.*
2)	....
3)	....

A: I was wondering if I could borrow your vacuum cleaner.
B: Of course. Go right ahead!

B *Pair work*

Student B: You're moving to a new apartment. You want your friend (Student A) to help you. Write your requests in the box below. Then ask your friend for help.

Student A: Accept or decline your friend's (Student B's) requests.

1)	*Is it OK if I borrow these boxes?*
2)	....
3)	....

8 WHAT DID THEY SAY?

Watch the video and complete the conversation. Then practice it.

Abby asks her friend Renee for a favor.

Abby: Renee? I am so .... you're there. I was
.... if you could help me out.
Renee: .... ?
Abby: I .... to ask a big .... My ....
just called, and he wants me to go out of town ....
.... to meet with a client.
Renee: .... ! You wanted to .... with more clients.
Abby: Yeah. But the problem is my .... are out of
town and my little sister is .... with me for
the ....
Renee: Hmm, that *is* a ....
Abby: Yeah, that's why I'm .... if she stayed
with you? It would only be for .... I'll pick her up ....
.... by ten o'clock.
Renee: No, I .... at all. But .... you .... her to ....
something to entertain herself while I .... on my .... ?
Abby: Sure, ...

---

9 INDIRECT REQUESTS *Asking favors*

A Abby has asked Renee to look after her apartment while she is away.
Abby has several requests for Renee. Complete their phone conversation
with the correct form of the expressions in the box.

Abby: Would you mind *..taking.in.the.mail.every.day...* ?
Renee: Sure, no problem. I'll leave it on the table.
Abby: Great. And could you .... ?
Renee: I'd love to. I've got some fish at home.
Abby: And let's see. I was wondering if you could
.... ?
Renee: Sure. I'll write them on your notepad.
Abby: Great. Oh, and I was wondering if you'd mind
.... ?
Renee: Yeah, I guess. How often does he need a walk?
Abby: Only three times a day. Anyway, one more thing. Is it OK if Kathy
.... ?
Renee: Are you kidding? Of course it's OK. Kathy and I get along just fine.

feed the fish
spend the weekend
✔ take in the mail every day
take phone messages
walk the dog

B *Pair work* Imagine you are going away for a weekend, and your
partner is going to look after your apartment or house. Write several
requests. Then take turns asking each other the favors.

13

4 Bigfoot lives!

1 CULTURE

North Americans enjoy telling stories. Scary or mysterious stories are popular around the campfire, at slumber parties, and during the fall and winter months, especially near Halloween. People tell and listen to stories about spirits, ghosts, and monsters as a way of dealing with their fear of the unknown, and because they can pretend to feel afraid while knowing they are really safe with their friends.

Do you enjoy telling and listening to stories? Do you enjoy scary stories? Why or why not? Are stories about spirits or monsters popular in your culture? If you can, share a well-known story from your culture with some classmates.

2 VOCABULARY Descriptions

For each pair of pictures write the correct description.

1)

an incredible story   *a ridiculous story*

a ridiculous story
an incredible story

2)

a mysterious situation
a scary situation

3)

a growl
a howl

4)

an encounter
a sighting

14

3 GUESS THE STORY

Watch the first two and a half minutes of the video with the sound off.
These young women have heard a story about a monster in the woods. Who do you think believes the story? Give reasons for your answers.

Amy

Beth

Cristina

 **Watch the video**

4 GET THE PICTURE

A Check your answers to Exercise 3. Did you guess correctly?

B Check (✔) **True** or **False**. Correct the false statements. Then compare with a partner.

	True	*False*	
1) Amy encounters Bigfoot on a path and tells the others.	☐	☐	....
2) Beth sees the "real" Bigfoot on her way to the bathhouse.	☐	☐	....
3) Amy shows Beth some tracks.	☐	☐	....
4) Cristina discovers Amy's trick.	☐	☐	....

5 WATCH FOR DETAILS

Complete the sentences. Then compare your answers with a partner.

1) There have been Bigfoot sightings all over the United States and ......*Canada*...... .

2) Beth goes to the bathhouse to ....

3) Cristina doesn't think the creature likes ....

4) Beth drops her .... when she hears Bigfoot.

5) Cristina thinks the noise was made by ....

6) Amy shows Beth .... from Bigfoot.

7) Cristina finds .... in the bushes.

6 MAKING INFERENCES

A How do the women feel? Match an adjective with a picture.

angry	apologetic	disbelieving	excited	nervous	surprised

....

....

B *Pair work* Take turns telling about times when you have felt the emotions in part A.

A: I felt very nervous the first time I heard a ghost story.
B: Really? I felt very excited.

Follow-up

7 DO YOU BELIEVE THESE STORIES?

Group work Read the descriptions of the creatures below. Do you believe they ever existed? Do you think they exist now? Have conversations like this:

A: Do you think the Loch Ness Monster exists?
B: I think it's just a story. There are no such things as monsters!
C: I hate to disagree, but there have been plenty of sightings.

The Loch Ness Monster, Scotland

Alien Big Cats, England

This creature was first seen in 565 A.D., and sightings are still reported every year. Some people believe that it is a dinosaur, an eel, or a type of whale. Many photos of "Nessie" have been taken, but some have turned out to be fakes and others are too dark or blurry to really show the creature.

Some people believe that large, wild cats, such as panthers and leopards, exist in some areas of the English countryside. Called "alien" because they are foreign (not extraterrestrial!), none has ever been captured. Photos and videos have never been clear enough to prove their existence, yet there were over 600 sightings in 1999 alone.

Language close-up

8 WHAT DID THEY SAY?

Watch the video and complete the conversation. Then practice it.

Cristina and Beth find out Amy played a trick on them.

Amy: You don't think *I* did it!

Cristina: I do. First, ... you told us .... Bigfoot, you .... a bearskin and tape recorder .... in the woods. Then, when Beth .... to take a shower, you .... to get some .... to toast the marshmallows. You were .... when Beth had her .... with Bigfoot.

Amy: That was .... a coincidence!

Cristina: Was it? You .... with us when Beth and I went to get her .... and things. After we left, you had .... of time to reset the .... and to make the .... before we ....

Beth: Aha! Busted!

Amy: You're .... good, Cristina. I .... I'd get ....

9 PAST TENSE VERBS *Telling a story*

A Write the correct form of the verbs in parentheses (past perfect, past continuous, or simple past) to complete this story of a mysterious sighting.

In December of 1950, mountain-climbing guide Sen Tensing .... (come) down a mountain path in Nepal when he and his friends .... (see) a hairy creature in the snow. The men .... (hide) behind a rock. When Sen Tensing .... (come out), after the creature .... (disappear) back down the trail, he found giant footprints the creature .... (leave) in the snow. Nearly a year later, Sen Tensing and two English mountain climbers .... (find) more large tracks while they .... (explore) the area around Mt. Everest. The men believed these tracks .... (be made) by a *yeti*, which some people think is a relative of Bigfoot. Or is there another explanation?

B *Pair work*

A: Imagine that you saw the Loch Ness Monster, an Alien Big Cat, or another creature. Tell a story.

B: Listen and ask questions. Then change roles.

5 Travel World

1 CULTURE

Culture shock, the emotional and physical distress you may feel when you visit a foreign country or culture, has three stages. The first stage, sometimes called the "honeymoon" stage, is characterized by exaggerated happiness and excitement. In the second stage, you might feel angry or sad at not being able to communicate or understand the other culture. You might even get physically ill. Finally, in the third stage, you realize that the new culture offers rewards as well as challenges, and you feel ready and able to adapt to a new lifestyle.

Have you ever experienced culture shock? Describe your experiences.
Have you ever seen a visitor to your country experiencing culture shock?
What kind of person do you think experiences culture shock the most severely? the least severely? What would you do if you thought you were experiencing culture shock?

2 VOCABULARY *Travel abroad*

Put the words below in the word map. Add at least one more word to each list. Then compare answers with a partner.

beautiful	embarrassed	shaking hands
confused	kissing in public	spectacular
eating a huge meal at lunch	picturesque	uncomfortable

Customs
....
....
....
....
....

TRAVEL ABROAD

Feelings
....
....
....
....

Scenery
....
....
....
....

3 GUESS THE FACTS

What things do you think cause people to experience culture shock?
Check (✔) your guesses.

☐ climate   ☐ dating customs   ☐ greetings   ☐ language

☐ clothing   ☐ food   ☐ hotels   ☐ transportation

 **Watch the video**

4 GET THE PICTURE

A Check your answers from Exercise 3. Then compare with a partner.

B Complete the information for each person.

Camilla
Lives in: ....
Visited: ....

Mônica
Is from: ....
Visited: ....

Sally
Is from: ....
Lives in: ....

Andrew
Is from: ....
Lives in: ....

Monie
Is from: ....
Lives in: ....

Delfino
Is from: ....
Lives in: ....

5 WATCH FOR DETAILS

According to the video, to which country do the following customs refer?
Write the name of a country next to each custom.

Brazil   Peru   Sweden
Mexico   the Philippines   the United States

1) People shake hands when they meet. ....

2) Couples kiss in public. ....

3) It's customary to eat a huge meal around noon. ....

4) Casual dress for teachers is acceptable in a university. ....

5) It's unacceptable to kiss in public. ....

6) People kiss on the cheek when they meet. ....

6 WHAT'S YOUR OPINION?

A Which customs and situations discussed in the video would make you feel uncomfortable
when visiting a foreign country? Rank them from 1 to 6 (1 = most uncomfortable).

.... seeing couples kissing in public   .... dressing professionally to teach in school

.... frequent earthquakes   .... greeting someone by kissing on the cheeks

.... using public transportation   .... eating a huge meal in the middle of the day

B *Pair work* Take turns talking about the customs. Use sentences like these:

One thing I'd be most uncomfortable about . . .   The thing that I'd be most uncomfortable about . . .
Something I wouldn't be uncomfortable about . . .   The thing that I'd be least uncomfortable about . . .

 **Follow-up**

7 CROSSING CULTURES

A Choose a country you know well. Make a list of customs that visitors to that
country might find different or unusual. Complete the chart.

Country	Customs	
....	....	....
	....	....

B *Pair work* Take turns asking about the customs in the countries you and your
partner chose in part A.

Language close-up

8 WHAT DID HE SAY?

Watch the video to complete the commentary. Then compare with a partner.

Chris Brooks talks about culture shock.

Hi. I'm Chris Brooks. .... to *Travel World*. Have you ever
.... to a .... with a ....
different ....? If you have, you .... know what
"............................ ...." is. It's a feeling of ....
you get from .... being in a new ....
The .... and .... may seem ....
.... are different. You don't know exactly what you're
.... do. You may .... be a little ....
.... of making a .... In .... , you get ....
.... everything. But .... you get .... , you often have some
.... and perhaps .... stories to ....
about your .... experiences.

9 EXPECTATIONS *Describing customs*

Read the notes that Camilla and Mônica made on their trips to Sweden
and Japan. Then use the phrases below to write advice they would give
to friends visiting these countries.

You're (not)
expected to . . .

You're (not)
supposed to . . .

It's (not)
acceptable to . . .

It's (not)
customary to . . .

Camilla's notes

In Sweden:
- *Be punctual!*
- *At formal dinners, don't drink until the host has made a toast.*
- *Don't engage in emotional arguments.*
- *Bring a cake to work on your birthday.*

Mônica's notes

In Japan:
- *Take off your shoes before entering someone's home.*
- *Don't use soap in the bathtub!*
- *Bow when you meet someone.*
- *Don't eat in public.*

1) *In Sweden, you're expected to be punctual.* ....

2) ....

3) ....

4) ....

5) ....

6) ....

7) ....

8) ....

6 Heartbreak Hotel

1 CULTURE

Travelers in North America looking for quaint, old-fashioned charm or personalized service sometimes choose to stay in a bed and breakfast, or "B & B." Herb and Ruth Boven opened Castle in the Country in Allegan, Michigan, in 1990. "Our guests come here to relax, enjoy the countryside, or shop at antique markets and specialty shops," says Ruth. Castle in the Country offers special mystery or romance weekends and services such as horse-drawn wagon rides and holiday dinners. "We enjoy meeting guests from different states and countries and showing them what's special about our area."

Have you ever stayed in a B & B? Would you like to stay in one? Talk about different types of hotels in your country with your classmates.

2 VOCABULARY Problems

Complete the sentences with words from the box. Then match each sentence with a picture. Compare with a partner.

cracked	scratched
✔dirty	stained
freezing	stuck
peeling	wrinkled

1) The room needs cleaning. It's very ......*dirty*...... .

2) The paint is coming off the walls. It's ....

3) Oh, no. I spilled jam on my shirt. Now it's ....

4) The cat jumped on my CD. It's ....

5) The cup is broken. It's ....

6) I can't open the window. It's ....

7) My clothes need to be ironed. They are ....

8) The temperature control is broken. It's .... in here.

3 GUESS THE STORY

Check (✔) what you think is happening in each of the following situations.
Then compare with a partner.

☐ A guest is checking out.

☐ The manager is leaving.

☐ The couple is here to relax.

☐ The couple is here on business.

☐ The couple likes the room.

☐ The couple doesn't like the room.

 **Watch the video**

4 GET THE PICTURE

Complete the chart. Check (✔) the word that describes each problem.
More than one answer may be possible.

	broken	dirty	peeling	scratched	stuck
1) temperature control	☐	☐	☐	☐	☐
2) paint	☐	☐	☐	☐	☐
3) furniture	☐	☐	☐	☐	☐
4) window	☐	☐	☐	☐	☐
5) carpet	☐	☐	☐	☐	☐

5 WATCH FOR DETAILS

Complete the sentences with **Mike**, **Walt**, **Kim**, or **Eddie**.

1) .... needs to run some errands.

2) .... likes quaint little hotels more than big, fancy ones.

3) .... found the hotel on the Internet.

4) .... checks the couple into the hotel.

5) .... calls the front desk to report a problem.

6) .... tries to repair the window.

7) .... tries to make some tea.

8) .... returns after the guests leave.

6 WHAT'S YOUR OPINION?

Pair work Answer these questions.

1) Do you agree with Kim and Mike's decision to check out of the hotel? What would you have done?

2) Think of an experience you've had where there were problems. Tell your partner about the problems and what you did to solve them.

 Follow-up

7 ROLE PLAY *Describe the problems*

A *Pair work* How many problems can you find in the picture below? Take turns describing the problems to each other.

B *Group work* Now join another pair. Three of you are customers. The fourth person is the waiter.

Customers: Complain to the waiter about the problems in the restaurant.
Waiter: Offer solutions to the customers' complaints.

Start like this:
Customer 1: Excuse me, but our dinners are cold.
Waiter: Oh, I'm sorry. I'll take them back and heat them up.
Customer 2: OK. That would be fine.
Customer 3: Actually, could I order something else instead?

 **Language close-up**

8 WHAT DID THEY SAY?

Watch the video and complete the conversation. Then practice it.

Mike and Kim complain to Eddie about their room.

Mike: We are .... !
Eddie: Is there something the .... ?
Mike: ....'s the matter! First of all,
        the .... control is still ....
Kim: The room was .... Now it's .... ,
        and we can't .... the heat.
Mike: The window is .... – again. Now we can't .... it.
Kim: There's no .... , and even the ....
        doesn't work.
Mike: In fact, ... works! Everything is in need of
        .... I want to see the ....
Eddie: Of course, sir. Just a ....
Mike: Can you .... this place? What .... can go wrong?
Eddie: What .... is the .... , folks?

9 NEED *WITH PASSIVE INFINITIVES AND GERUNDS*
Describing problems

A Read the list of additional problems at the hotel that Eddie needs to fix. Then
write two sentences with *need* for each problem. Use the verbs in the box.

Eddie's List	
☐ the heat is stuck on high	☐ the hair dryer is broken
☐ the wastebasket is full	☐ the rooms are dirty
☐ the chair is damaged	☐ the floors are dirty

✔adjust	fix
clean	repair
empty	wash

1) *The heat needs adjusting./The heat needs to be adjusted.* ....

2) ....

3) ....

4) ....

5) ....

6) ....

B Now think of two things that need to be done at your school or at your
home. Then write two sentences to describe what needs to be done.

1) ....

2) ....

7 Saving Florida's manatees

 **Preview**

1 CULTURE

State and national parks play an important role in preserving North America's wildlife and its natural habitat. Parks offer large areas of wilderness where plants and animals can live undisturbed. Some parks rehabilitate injured animals or breed endangered animals, and then release them into the wild. In addition, park rangers offer educational programs for visitors to learn about and see wildlife. Park museums feature exhibits for both adults and children to learn more about wildlife and the importance of protecting natural resources.

Talk about national parks that you have visited or know about. What are they famous for? What can you see there? What kinds of plants and animals live there? What kinds of animals would you be interested in seeing in parks in your country or another country?

2 VOCABULARY *Environment*

Pair work Match the words in the box with one of the pictures. Then use the word in a sentence describing the picture.

conservation	natural environment	pollution
development	✔predator	refuge

1) ....

2) ....

3) ....

4) ....

5) *predator* ....

6) ....

3 GUESS THE FACTS

Which of the following do you think are threats to the manatee?
Check (✔) your guesses.

☐ boats   ☐ disease   ☐ global warming   ☐ pollution
☐ development   ☐ fishing lines   ☐ hunters   ☐ predators

 **Watch the video**

4 GET THE PICTURE

A Look at your answers to Exercise 3. Did you guess correctly? Correct your answers.
Then compare with a partner.

B What are the organizations in Florida doing to help the manatees? Match what
the organizations do with their picture.

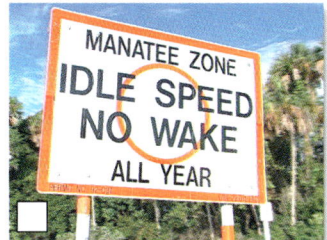         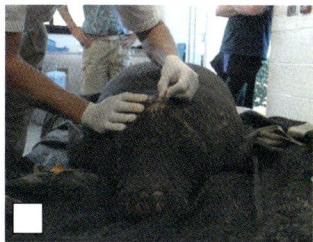

Crystal River National   Homosassa Springs   Florida Marine   SeaWorld®
Wildlife Refuge   Wildlife Park   Research Institute

1) They study places wild manatees swim to   3) They provide a natural warm-water habitat
    in summer months.   for manatees in the winter.

2) They rescue and help injured manatees.   4) They teach visitors how manatees are being
                                                      threatened.

5 WATCH FOR DETAILS

Fill in the blanks. Then compare with a partner.

1) Manatees evolved more than .... million years ago.

2) The average adult male manatee weighs about .... pounds and can
   eat up to .... percent of its body weight in aquatic plants each day.

3) Manatees have a normal life span of .... years or more.

4) During the last survey, only .... were counted in the United States.

5) The Crystal River National Wildlife Refuge covers .... acres.

6) Manatees must breathe when they are active during the day every ....
   to .... minutes.

7) For more than .... years, Dr. Buddy Powell has been studying manatees.

6 GUESSING MEANING FROM CONTEXT

Read these sentences from the video. Guess the meanings of the underlined words.
Check (✔) your answers. Then compare with a partner.

1) What's left of the manatees' natural habitat may be <u>contaminated</u> by pollution.

   ☐ made dirty   ☐ increased   ☐ improved

2) Manatees, like people, will die of <u>hypothermia</u> if left in cold water for too long.

   ☐ pollution   ☐ lack of food   ☐ low body temperature

3) Another sign to look for is the manatee's <u>snout</u>, as it comes to the surface to breathe.

   ☐ nose   ☐ tail   ☐ noise

4) Information they gather will help policy makers develop better <u>strategies</u> for protecting the manatee in the future.

   ☐ areas   ☐ plans   ☐ scientists

5) Here at SeaWorld® in Orlando, teams work to <u>nurse</u> manatees <u>back</u> to good health.

   ☐ feed   ☐ experiment   ☐ restore

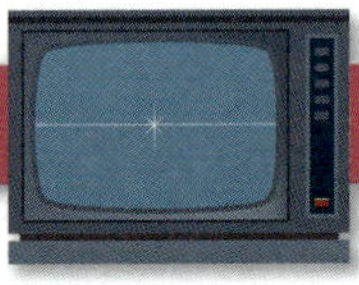

Follow-up

7 A CONSERVATION PLAN

snow leopard    bald eagle    giant panda    rhinoceros    gorilla

A *Pair work* Imagine you are planning a program to help an endangered or threatened animal. Choose an animal and list your plans to help save it.

Animal	*Plans for conservation*
....	....
	....
	....
	....

B *Group work* Now join another group. Take turns presenting your ideas. Use expressions like these:

One thing to do is to create a wildlife refuge.   An important thing to do is to . . .
The best way to solve this problem is to . . .   Another way to help is to . . .

Language close-up

8 WHAT DID THEY SAY?

Watch the video to complete the commentaries. Then compare with a partner.

The importance of saving the manatees is explained.

Narrator: So why is it .... to continue to spend
so much .... and .... on this seemingly
insignificant creature? .... it has to do with
our own well-being.

Man: I think they're kind of like a .... of how the
....'s doing. And if manatees can
.... alongside us, I think our environment's
going to be doing ....

Woman 1: We're not only providing and .... habitat
for a .... species, but we're also ....
a healthy habitat for ....

Woman 2: .... the ones that .... do something about it;
otherwise, our .... and their children might
not see ....

9 PASSIVE; PREPOSITIONS OF CAUSE
Describing environmental problems and solutions

Rewrite these sentences from the active to the passive. Use the prepositions in parentheses to indicate the cause. Then compare with a partner.

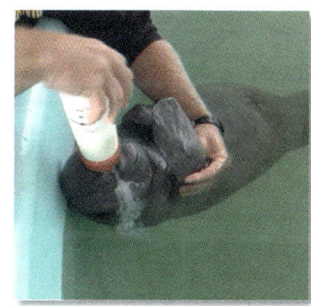

1) The work of volunteers all over the world is helping injured and endangered animals. (as a result of)

   Injured and endangered animals are being helped as a result
   of the work of volunteers all over the world.

2) Stricter controls for watercraft are improving the quality of life for some manatees. (through)

   ....
   ....

3) Development has reduced the habitat of many wild animals. (because of)

   ....
   ....

4) Fast-moving watercraft have injured a large number of manatees. (by)

   ....
   ....

5) Exhaust from cars and smoke from factories have contaminated the air. (due to)

   ....
   ....

8 Salsa!

Preview

1 CULTURE

Salsa music and dance began in New York City around the 1930s. Musicians from Caribbean islands such as Puerto Rico and Cuba moved to New York and encountered Latin American and African American music. The resulting blend evolved into the salsa we hear today. It's no surprise that salsa, with such a mixed background, is popular in so many different areas of the world. And salsa music hasn't stopped evolving; today you can even hear techno-salsa and salsa rap. Who can predict the next direction that salsa will take?

Why do you think people like to dance? Give as many reasons as you can.
What kinds of dances are popular in your country? What kinds have you tried?
What kinds of music are popular in your country now?

2 VOCABULARY Learning

A *Pair work* What are some phrases used to talk about learning? Match the verbs on the left to a word or phrase on the right.

1) decide to ⟍⟍⟍⟍⟍ to ski
2) earn ⟋ take lessons
3) brush up on hitting the ball
4) learn how a diploma
5) practice classes
6) take my skills

B Complete the sentences below with phrases from part A. Change the verb form if necessary.

1) I heard you're interested in playing the violin. Did you
   decide to take lessons ?

2) If you want to get better at tennis, you'll have to .... !

3) I already know how to do karate, but I'm taking lessons just to ....

4) It's hard to learn to dance by myself. I'm going to .... with a friend.

5) Kim graduated from college last May. She .... in engineering.

6) This winter, James wants to ....

3 GUESS THE FACTS

Why do you think salsa dancing is so popular?
What are some ways people learn or improve salsa dancing?

 **Watch the video**

4 GET THE PICTURE

What reasons do people give for why salsa is popular? Check (✔) your answers.
Then compare with a partner.

☐ It's easy to do.

☐ The music is enjoyable.

☐ Lessons are not expensive.

☐ It's a mix of many trends and cultures.

☐ It's a good way to meet people.

☐ You don't have to learn many steps.

5 WATCH FOR DETAILS

How do these people recommend learning or improving salsa dancing?
Match each person with a recommendation.

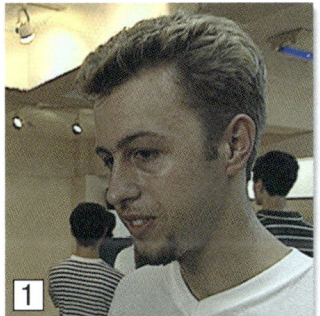

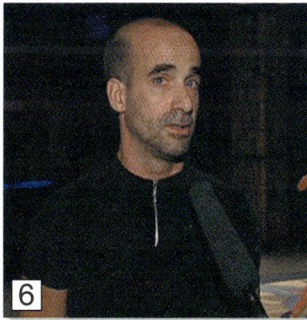

☐ By moving to the music.

☐ By coming to class every weekend.

☐ By taking the initiative.

☐ By practicing with a partner.

☐ By practicing hard.

☐ By going out to nightclubs and getting together with friends at parties.

6 WHAT'S YOUR OPINION?

A How important do you think these qualities are for learning how to dance?
Number them from 1 (most important) to 9 (least important).

☐ athletic ability   ☐ curiosity   ☐ patience

☐ competitiveness   ☐ intelligence   ☐ self-confidence

☐ creativity   ☐ motivation   ☐ willpower

B *Pair work* Compare your answers with a partner. Explain how you made
your choices. Then talk about these activities. Would your rankings change?
Why or why not?

learning a foreign language   learning how to play tennis   learning how to cook

Follow-up

7 ADVICE TO LEARNERS

A Think of a sport, game, or activity that you have learned.
Make a list of different ways to learn it.

Activity ....

Ways to learn

....

....

....

....

....

....

....

....

....

B *Group work* Take turns asking and answering questions about the activities
the group members have chosen. Use language like this:

How did you learn to . . . ?   I learned . . . by . . .
Why do you enjoy . . . ?   I enjoy . . . because . . .
What's the best way to learn . . . ?   The best way to learn . . . is by . . .
What's a good way to improve . . . ?   A good way to improve . . . is to . . .

Language close-up

8 WHAT DID THEY SAY?

Watch the video to complete the conversation. Then practice with a partner.

A woman talks about learning salsa dancing.

Billy: You seem to be .... yourself. Do you come
here .... ?

Woman 5: Yes. I come here just about .... week. I come here
to ....

Billy: Why do you .... salsa is so .... ?

Woman 5: You don't .... a set of .... You just
.... to the music and ....
the music.

Billy: What's the best .... to learn salsa .... ? Any
.... ?

Woman 5: .... on how you .... Some
.... learn best by going to a .... I learn
best by .... and listening to the music and then
getting .... and .... it a little.

Billy: Do you .... taking lessons in a .... or
.... out to a club?

Woman 5: I prefer .... to a club and dancing here. There's a different
.... ; it's more .... But there's nothing
.... with taking lessons. I .... it.

9 GERUNDS AND INFINITIVES *Talking about preferences*

A For each pair of expressions complete the questions.

1) earn a diploma / learn for fun
Would you prefer *to earn a diploma or learn for fun* .... ?

2) learn English in Australia / learn English in Canada
Would you rather .... ?

3) learn how to cook / learn how to dance salsa
Would you prefer .... ?

4) brush up on skills you already have / learn something new
Would you rather .... ?

5) read English magazines / read English novels
Would you rather .... ?

6) study in the morning / study at night
Would you prefer .... ?

B **Group work** Ask several classmates the questions in part A.
Then share their answers with the class.

Mari would prefer to start a business. Juan would rather learn to dance at home.

9 Stress relief

1 CULTURE

What is stress? There are three main types:
1) Mechanical stress, which can be caused by carrying heavy objects, not getting enough exercise, or sleep disorders.
2) Mental stress, caused by things such as relationship problems, financial worries, or career concerns.
3) Chemical stress, caused by air and water pollution, detergents and cleaning products, and chemicals used in manufacturing.
Our bodies react to stress with the "fight or flight" response; you may want to challenge what stresses you, or you may want to run away!

What other kinds of mechanical, mental, and chemical stresses can you think of?
Make a list with a partner or group. How many of these do you think affect you?
What are some solutions to stress? What is your favorite way to relax?

2 VOCABULARY Stress

Choose from the expressions in the box to complete the paragraph below.
Each expression is used only once.

blow off steam	✔ stressed out	take some time off	under pressure
has got to stop	the right thing for me	take up	you can say that again

Last year, I felt so ...*stressed out*... by my job. Every day it seemed
like I was .... from my boss. I
used to .... by complaining to
my co-workers, but that didn't work – it only made them feel stressed,
too! One day, someone in my office brought me a brochure from a health
club. "This complaining .... ,"
she said. "Why don't you ....
from work and .... exercising?"
It turned out to be just .... My
co-workers were so happy about how relaxed I was when I came back.
They told me never to forget how important it is to take care of myself.
.... !

3 GUESS THE STORY

Watch the first minute of the video with the sound off.
Answer these questions.

1) What is the woman's problem?
2) What do you think the man is telling her?

 **Watch the video**

4 GET THE PICTURE

A Check (✔) the suggestions for stress relief that John offers Margie.

☐ aromatherapy

☐ ice-skating

☐ taking a trip

☐ dance lessons

☐ sleeping

☐ talking to friends

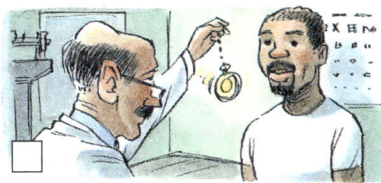

☐ hypnotherapy

☐ swimming

☐ yoga

B *Pair work* Which of the activities above have you tried? Which would you like to try?

5 WATCH FOR DETAILS

Why doesn't Margie like these suggestions for stress relief? Check (✔)
the reason Margie rejects each suggestion.

1) Rollerblading®	☐ She got hurt.	☐ Lessons were too expensive.
2) dance lessons	☐ She broke her toe.	☐ She couldn't find a good partner.
3) swimming	☐ She can't swim.	☐ The pool was too crowded.
4) yoga class	☐ It's probably not the right thing for her.	☐ She's already tried it.
5) hypnotherapy	☐ It didn't work.	☐ It worked too well.
6) aromatherapy	☐ Perfumes make her sleepy.	☐ Perfume makes her sneeze.

6 WHAT'S YOUR OPINION?

A *Pair work* Imagine that John suggests these activities for reducing stress to Margie. Write the reasons Margie might give for rejecting them.

playing tennis
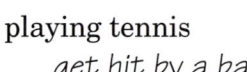
...get hit by a ball........

running
....

listening to music
....

doing aerobics
....

B *Pair work* Now act out John and Margie's conversation. Start like this:
John: Have you thought about playing tennis?
Margie: I've already tried that, but I got hit by the ball!

Follow-up

7 HOW STRESSED ARE YOU?

A *Pair work* How much stress do you feel in the situations below? Add one more idea and check (✔) your answers. Then compare with a partner. Have conversations like this:

A: How much stress do you feel at school?
B: A lot. I have too much homework every night. How about you?

	none at all	a little	some	a lot
1) at school or work	☐	☐	☐	☐
2) with friends	☐	☐	☐	☐
3) on weekends	☐	☐	☐	☐
4) when visiting your relatives	☐	☐	☐	☐
5) when traveling	☐	☐	☐	☐
6) .... (your idea)	☐	☐	☐	☐

B *Class activity* Ask your classmates about how much stress they feel in the situations. Check (✔) their answers in the chart. Which things are the most stressful? the least stressful?

8 WHAT DID THEY SAY?

Watch the video and complete the conversation. Then practice it.

Margie explains her problem to John.

Margie: Ah! This has .... stop.

John: What is it, Margie? You look so ....

Margie: John, it's this .... I'm under .... all
          the time. My muscles are .... My stomach is
          .... I just can't seem to .... What can I do?

John: Yeah, ... It's a .... Well, one ....
          you could do is exercise. It really .... me when I'm
          .... , and it's a great way to ....
          .... steam.

Margie: Well, ... , I've tried that. .... I took up Rollerblading®, . . .
          but that .... Then I tried .... lessons, . . . but I
          couldn't find a good dance ....

9 SUGGESTIONS

A John would like some advice for his problems. Write a suggestion
for each of his problems. Use the expressions in the box.

| Why don't you . . . ? | What about . . . ? | It might be a good idea to . . . |
| Maybe you could . . . ? | Have you thought about . . . ? | One thing you could do is . . . |

1) I'd really like to learn Spanish, but I never seem to have enough time.

....

2) Sometimes I can't finish my work because I get too many phone calls.

....

3) I want to go on vacation next month, but the boss wants me to be in the office.

....

4) I'd like to do something interesting on my lunch hour.

....

5) I love to read at night, but I usually fall asleep as soon as I begin to read.

....

B *Pair work* Write two problems you have for which you would like advice.
Then take turns reading your problems and offering suggestions.

1) ....

2) ....

10 Fort Steele Heritage Town

1 CULTURE

Living historic villages are towns that have been restored to show a certain period in history. Workers dress up in costumes of that period and take on traditional roles and reenact daily life from long ago. Visitors can walk through old-time homes, schools, and shops. Historic villages preserve traditional arts and antiques, give demonstrations of traditional crafts, reenact historic events, and educate visitors about the times and people of a particular region.

Talk about countries whose history interests you. What time periods do you know about? Which would you like to learn more about? If you could visit a living historic village from any time period, what would you like to see?

2 VOCABULARY *Life long ago*

Match the word in the box to the correct picture below.

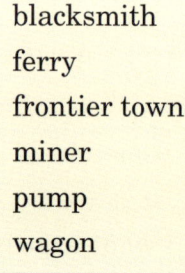

blacksmith
ferry
frontier town
miner
pump
wagon

....

....

3 GUESS THE FACTS

Why do you think settlers from eastern Canada and the United States moved west in the late 1800s?

Watch the video

4 GET THE PICTURE

A What job at Fort Steele does each person have? Match each job with a person.

1) schoolteacher   3) mountie   5) short-distance hauler
2) general manager   4) blacksmith

B Which job is described? Write a job from part A next to each phrase.

.... taught grades 1 through 8 together in two rooms

.... solved problems through words, not violence

.... built and repaired tools

.... would like to add more tradespeople to Fort Steele

.... led an animal that carried heavy objects

5 WATCH FOR DETAILS

Check (✔) **True** or **False**. Then correct the false statements. Compare with a partner.

	True	False	
1) Fort Steele is located in eastern Canada.	☐	✔	*It is located in western Canada.*
2) Fort Steele started as a ferry crossing.	☐	☐	....
3) Fort Steele closed because a railroad was built through a neighboring town.	☐	☐	....
4) For more than 100 years the town was deserted.	☐	☐	....
5) Fort Steele Heritage Town was started by railroad employees.	☐	☐	....
6) Fort Steele Heritage Town was started in 1961.	☐	☐	....
7) Fort Steele residents did not have electricity.	☐	☐	....
8) In the future, more visitors will probably be coming to Fort Steele Heritage Town.	☐	☐	....
9) New attractions that might be added to Heritage Town are a tinsmith and a harness maker.	☐	☐	....

6 MAKING INFERENCES

Pair work Think about what you saw in the video and make guesses about what life was like in Fort Steele in the 1890s. Discuss your ideas with a partner.

1) How did people wash clothes?
2) Where did they get their food from?
3) What did people use for transportation?
4) What did they use animals for?
5) What were their houses made of?

 **Follow-up**

7 CREATE A LIVING HISTORIC VILLAGE

A *Pair work* Choose one of the following periods in English history, or a time from your country's history, and imagine you are going to create a living historic village to explain what life was like then. What kinds of things would you show and explain? Make a list.

Medieval period
twelfth century

Elizabethan period
late sixteenth century

Victorian period
mid-nineteenth century

Living Historic Village ....

Things to show and explain:
1) ....
2) ....
3) ....
4) ....
5) ....
6) ....

B *Group work* Get together with another pair to explain the plan for your living historic village. Ask questions about each other's villages like this:

Will you sell souvenirs? Will you show the inside of people's homes?

8 WHAT DID HE SAY?

Watch the video to complete the commentary. Then compare with a partner.
The narrator explains the history of Fort Steele.

So, what was it .... in .... during the nineteenth
.........................? The late 1800s were a .... of westward
expansion and .... in Canada. Some people were
.... west, seeking their fortunes in the .... fields.
.... came to claim .... for farms and ....
The shopkeepers and tradesmen came soon after, offering ....
and .... to the new .... New

.... towns were born. Fort Steele was a ....
town of that .... It began as a .... crossing over the
Kootenay River, providing a way for .... to reach the gold
fields. Then, in .... , the Canadian Pacific Railway
.... their new rail line through the ....
town of Cranbrook. .... a few years, the ....
of Fort Steele was .... to a couple of hundred. .... more
than fifty years, the .... was deserted.

9 TALKING ABOUT THE PAST

A Use words from the box to complete the paragraph about
Prince Edward Island in Canada. Then compare with a partner.
Some prepositions are used more than once.

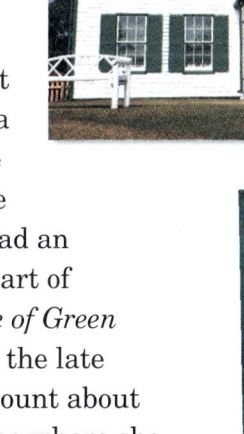

after	during	for	since
ago	from	in	to

Jacques Cartier of France was the first European to discover
Prince Edward Island over 450 years .... The first
French settlement was built .... 1719, and is now a
national historic site. .... the 1700s and 1880s, the
island was controlled at different times by the British and the
French. .... 1769 .... 1873, the island had an
independent government; .... then, it has been a part of
Canada. Lucy Montgomery, who wrote the popular novel *Anne of Green
Gables* .... 1908, lived on the island .... the late
1880s and early 1900s. *Anne of Green Gables* is a fictional account about
life on Prince Edward Island. Tourists today can visit the home where she
lived .... thirty-five years. .... touring the museum,
many visitors stop by the bookstore to purchase copies of her novels.

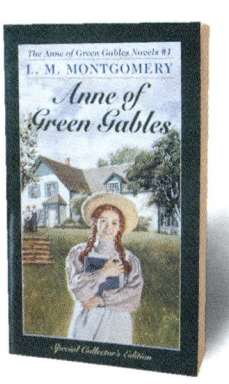

B *Group work*   Take turns telling your group about the history of a
famous place in your country. What can tourists see or do there today?

11 If only . . .

1 CULTURE

Most Americans are familiar with change. Consider these statistics:
- The typical American moves eleven times during his or her lifetime.
- The average employee changes jobs seven or eight times during his or her career.
- On average, college students change majors three to five times before graduation.
- In 1999, the most popular undergraduate majors were elementary education, business, psychology, pre-medicine, and computer science.

Tell your classmates how many times you have moved, changed your job, or changed your major. If you went to college, talk about what you studied and how you chose that field.

2 VOCABULARY *Behavior*

A Match the words in the box with the definitions below.

Someone who . . .
1) wants to be successful is ....*ambitious*........... .
2) works hard to achieve a goal is ....
3) has a lot of knowledge about the world is ....
4) sees things the way they really are is ....
5) doesn't joke or play around is ....
6) is practical, who always does the right thing is ....
7) has ideas that are too simple or unrealistic is ....
8) is easygoing, who doesn't worry much is ....

✔ ambitious
carefree
dedicated
naive
realistic
sensible
serious
sophisticated

B *Pair work* What qualities should you possess to do the following jobs? Use words from part A and ones of your own. Explain your choices to your partner.

Web designer

camp counselor

artist

small-business owner

3 GUESS THE STORY

Watch the first minute of the video with the sound off.
What are the women doing in each picture?

 **Watch the video**

4 GET THE PICTURE

Complete the chart. Fill in what each person is doing now.
Add one more piece of information.

Deanna

Pamela

Amelia

Laura

Roberta

Name	Now	Other
Deanna	successful lawyer	was always serious
Pamela		
Amelia		
Laura		
Roberta		

5 WATCH FOR DETAILS

Complete the chart. Check (✔) who the statements are about.

	Deanna	Pamela	Amelia	Laura	Roberta
1) She didn't study hard in college.	☐	☐	☐	☐	☐
2) She studied computers in college.	☐	☐	☐	☐	☐
3) She studied business in college.	☐	☐	☐	☐	☐
4) She didn't relax and have fun in college.	☐	☐	☐	☐	☐
5) She has traveled a lot.	☐	☐	☐	☐	☐
6) She acted in college.	☐	☐	☐	☐	☐
7) She graduated at the top of her class.	☐	☐	☐	☐	☐
8) She should have majored in languages.	☐	☐	☐	☐	☐

6 MAKING INFERENCES

Which statements are probably true? Which are probably false?
Check (✔) your answers. Then compare with a partner.

	True	False
1) The girls knew each other well in college.	☐	☐
2) In college, Deanna thought her friends weren't serious enough.	☐	☐
3) Pamela is more ambitious now than when she was in college.	☐	☐
4) Amelia's career goals have changed from when she was in college.	☐	☐
5) The girls think Amelia's plans are realistic.	☐	☐
6) In college, Roberta knew what she wanted to be.	☐	☐

 **Follow-up**

7 CHANGES

A *Pair work* Read the time line about Amelia's life. Take turns talking about the turning points in her life, like this:

A: Amelia was born in 1975.
B: By the time she started high school, her family had moved to California.

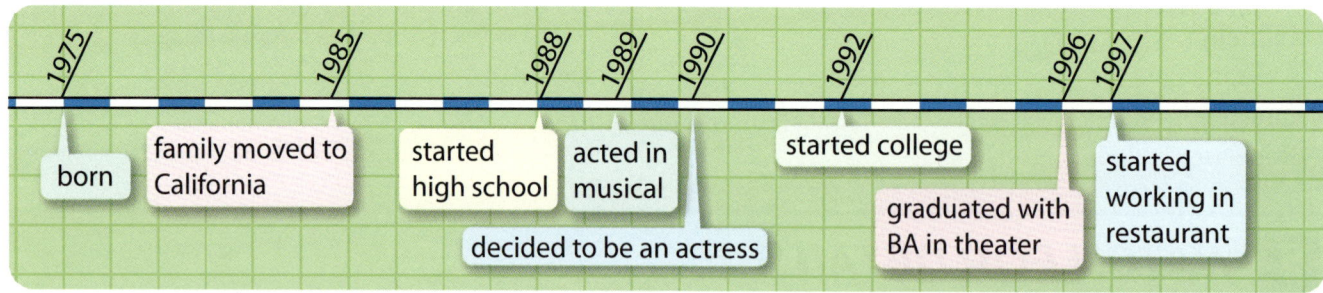

B Now make a time line similar to Amelia's about your life. Include six to eight turning points in your life on your time line.

C *Group work* Take turns sharing your time lines. Talk about what has happened in your life and how those changes affected you.

When I moved to California, I started watching a lot of movies. If I hadn't acted in a high school musical, I wouldn't have decided to become an actress. If I had majored in education in college, I might have gotten a better job, but I wouldn't have enjoyed myself so much.

Language close-up

8 WHAT DID THEY SAY?

Watch the video and complete the conversation. Then practice it.

Deanna and Pamela share their regrets.

Roberta: Oh, look at Deanna: always the .... one.
Amelia: Even then, you were .... at work.
Deanna: I know. I .... more carefree like
         the rest of you. I never .... to relax.
Laura: Oh, but you were so .... You always did well in
         school and .... at the top of your class.
Roberta: Yeah. Now .... at you. You are a .... lawyer.
Deanna: Yes, but I didn't think that .... a good time in college
         was .... The moment I graduated, I
         .... I .... a lot. I still don't know
         .... relax and have ....
Pamela: Well, Deanna, if I .... to you, I ....
         just a clerk at the office. .... the manager.

9 PAST CONDITIONALS

A Rewrite the sentences using **if** clauses + past perfect and the words given.

1) I should have studied harder.   (receive a scholarship)
   If I had studied harder, I might have received a scholarship.

2) You should have studied a foreign language.   (be able to study abroad)
   ....

3) We should have taken more summer classes.   (finish my degree earlier)
   ....

4) They should have been more ambitious.   (get better jobs)
   ....

5) She should have been more carefree.   (have more friends)
   ....

6)   He should have listened to his parents.   (make better decisions)
   ....

B *Group work* Talk about how your life would be different now if . . .

your parents had been millionaires.

you'd been born a member of the opposite sex.

you had lived 200 years ago.

you had never gone to school.

12 Need information? AskJeeves.com

1 CULTURE

Internet use is growing steadily in North America. In 1995, there were eighteen million Internet users; in just four years, that figure had grown to ninety-two million! The most popular reasons for using the Internet are sending and receiving e-mail (ninety percent of survey respondents), looking for general information (seventy-seven percent), and "surfing," or browsing through Web pages without any specific goal (sixty-nine percent). However, people also use the Internet for product and travel information, hobbies, work and business, playing games, job hunting, banking, and school homework.

Do you use the Internet? If so, tell what you use it for. What kinds of Web sites do you enjoy? What makes a Web site easy or difficult to use? How easy is it for you to find information on the Internet?

2 VOCABULARY   *The Internet*

A Complete the passage about the Internet with words from the box.

How do people use the Internet? First, ...*users*..... must .... , or connect their computer to the Internet. Then, once they're .... , they type in the .... of the page on the Internet they wish to visit. A few seconds later, they will see the .... appear on the screen. Some pages provide .... , which people can click on to visit related pages. When someone doesn't know which page would be most useful, he or she can use a .... to suggest different sites.

> links
> log on
> online
> search engine
> ✔users
> Web address
> Web site

B *Pair work* Take turns guessing the words in part A.
A: People who surf the Internet.
B: Users.

3 GUESS THE FACTS

What kind of a Web site do you think Ask Jeeves is?

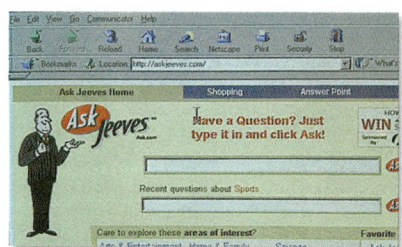

http://www.AskJeeves.com

46

 *Watch the video*

4 GET THE PICTURE

A Match the descriptions below to the correct pictures. Write the correct number in the box.

1) A group of interesting gentlemen help people and hand out free things.
2) The answer to your question is in the form of another question.
3) This character makes using the Internet a more human experience.
4) Companies pay to have their name on the Web site.

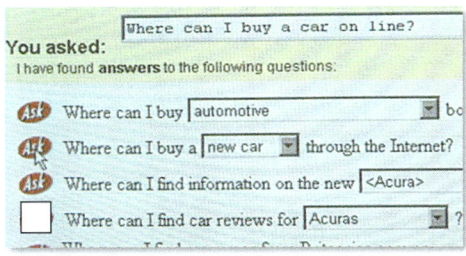

B Match these phrases to a picture above. Write a phrase under each picture.

a clever marketing idea   a revenue source
a good concept   a unique search engine

5 WATCH FOR DETAILS

Correct the mistakes below. Then compare with a partner.

The character of Jeeves, a helpful ~~librarian~~ *butler*, has been used in several marketing

campaigns. In the Butler Blast, a group of butlers is hired to attend events like

the opening of a mall. These gentlemen help people with their computers, give

directions, and hand out free things. Jeeves has also been a dancer in the Macy's

Thanksgiving Day Parade. Once, the company created labels for different

vegetables. The stickers included Jeeves's face and telephone number.

6 WHAT'S YOUR OPINION?

A Ask three of your classmates what they think about using the Internet for different purposes. Be sure to ask for reasons. Take notes in the chart.

	............(name)	............(name)	............(name)
1 Do you think it's a good idea to buy things over the Internet using a credit card?			
2 Would you rather send an e-mail message or a letter to your friend? Which would you rather receive?			
3 Is the Internet a good source of information about health?			
4 Is it easier for you to find information in the library or on the Internet?			
5 (your own question)			

B Share your information with the class. Did any comments surprise you?

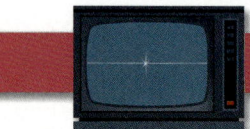 **Follow-up**

7 DESIGNING A WEB SITE

A *Pair work* Design a personal Web site or a Web site for a product, a hobby, or an interest. Plan the home page for your site. Draw your designed home page on a sheet of paper. Be sure to include important information and pictures.

B *Group work* Join another pair and take turns explaining your Web site.

Language close-up

8 WHAT DID THEY SAY?

Watch the video to complete the commentaries. Then compare with a partner.

Penny Finnie, Vice President of Ideas, and Marjorie Stout, Content Editor,
explain how the Ask Jeeves site is special.

Penny: Most .... , when they get on the .... ,
don't really .... where to go. And so they use ....
.... to find out what .... are out there in
their areas of .... Most search engines, you just
go and .... in one .... So if you
.... to buy a car, you .... type in *cars*. But what
comes .... is a long, long, long, long .... of all the car
sites .... With Jeeves, it's ....
Um, if you want to buy a car .... , you go and you
say, "Where can I buy a car online?" And Jeeves .... you
to the sites that .... that question.

Marjorie: Ask Jeeves is .... because it's .... a
question-and-answer .... You .... to Jeeves
and you ask a question. The answers we . . . we .... to
our .... are in the form of .... question. And
so you .... the question that Jeeves .... you that's
most .... to the one that you asked, and
.... that question is your answer.

---

9 INFINITIVE CLAUSES AND PHRASES OF PURPOSE
Advice for a successful Web site

Complete these sentences about advice for a Web site. Use **in order for** or **in order to**.

1) *In order for* .... the Web address to be easy to remember, it should
be short and interesting.

2) .... make the Web site more human, feature
an interactive character.

3) .... get users to come back again and again,
you need to update information frequently.

4) .... a Web site to generate revenue, it needs
to display advertising from other companies.

5) .... Web pages to be easily accessed, they
should have uncomplicated graphics.

Car trouble

1 CULTURE

Americans love their cars! Compared to their parents in the 1950s, people in the United States own twice as many cars and drive them twice as many miles. Today's average American drives 8,964 miles a year. Eighty-nine percent of American households own one or more cars. The driving age varies from state to state, but most Americans learn to drive in their midteens to late teens.

Do you or your family have a car? Tell a partner or group about it.
What are some advantages and disadvantages of owning a car?
Talk about other means of transportation you use regularly.

2 VOCABULARY *Car trouble*

Match statements from A with responses from B. Then compare with a partner and practice the statements and responses.

A	B
1) .... Nothing looked familiar! I had no idea where I was!	a) He could have taken a wrong turn.
2) .... We left the house at the same time. I wonder how my sister got to school ahead of me.	b) You might have run out of gas.
3) .... Carol stopped her car because smoke was coming out from under the hood!	c) She must have taken a shortcut.
4) .... My car slowed down and stopped completely. I called the garage.	d) You must have gotten lost.
5) .... He never found their house. He thought he followed the directions.	e) She might have had engine trouble.

3 GUESS THE STORY

Watch the first minute and a half of the video with the sound off.

Answer the questions.

1) Where are the men going?   2) What happened to them?   3) What might the women be thinking?

4 GET THE PICTURE

These are the things that happened to Sam and Bill. First put the pictures in order (1 to 5). Then write the correct sentence under each picture. Compare with a partner.

A farmer gives Sam and Bill a ride.
There's a "Road Closed" sign ahead.
Bill drives through a cornfield.

Sam goes to get water from the farmer.
Bill's car has engine trouble.

....

....

....

....

....

5 MAKING INFERENCES

A Which statements are probably true? Which are probably false? Check (✔) your answers. Then compare with a partner.

	True	False
1) Sam is a nervous person.	☐	☐
2) Debbie thinks the men will arrive on time.	☐	☐
3) Emily thinks the men may have had trouble.	☐	☐
4) Emily thinks Sam forgot about the photographer.	☐	☐
5) Debbie thinks Bill's car is reliable.	☐	☐
6) Bill is an optimistic person.	☐	☐

B *Pair work* Write two more statements and ask your partner if they are **probably true** or **probably false**.

6 WHAT'S YOUR OPINION?

A *Pair work* Complete the chart. Check (✔) the words that describe Bill, Sam, Emily, and Debbie.

	Bill	*Sam*	*Emily*	*Debbie*
carefree	☐	☐	☐	☐
reassuring	☐	☐	☐	☐
relaxed	☐	☐	☐	☐
sensible	☐	☐	☐	☐
stressed out	☐	☐	☐	☐
tense	☐	☐	☐	☐
upset	☐	☐	☐	☐
worried	☐	☐	☐	☐

B Do you know people like Bill, Sam, Emily, and Debbie? Talk about them like this:

A: My friend Tony is always relaxed. He is never stressed out.
B: He should meet my friend Alice. She's the most relaxed person I know.

Follow-up

7 WHAT'S YOUR ADVICE?

A Read these predicaments posted on a Web site.

> My sister called last night at 11 P.M. and wanted to talk. I didn't want to be rude, so I talked to her until 1 A.M. Today I was so tired, I fell asleep at work.

> My best friend and I were having a great time last night until we went to a party. That's when the fun stopped. She started acting differently to impress everyone. I was so embarrassed I wanted to leave, but I just stood there.

> One of my neighbors borrowed my new in-line skates about a month ago. He still hasn't returned them, even though I've asked him to several times. I don't want to start an argument, but I sure do miss skating.

B *Pair work* Take turns giving advice for each predicament. Say what the person could, should, or might have done. Then say what *you* would have done.

Lan **Language close-up**

8 WHAT DID THEY SAY?

Watch the video and complete the conversation. Then practice it.

Sam worries about getting to his wedding on time, while Bill reassures him.

Sam: We .... so much time at that gift shop.

Bill: Ah, I did the .... thing. The top of the wedding .... is everything!
Besides, this .... will get us .... with time to ....

Sam: I still think we .... on
Highway 41. Did you .... the ring? Bill, you did
not .... it?

Bill: .... It's right here. What time does the ....
begin?

Sam: ....

Bill: And .... is it now?

Sam: It's ....

Bill: Good! We have .... of time.

Sam: Yeah, but we have to be there an hour .... for pictures. That
only gives us .... an ....

Bill: .... me. We're almost there.

Sam: Except for that "................. ...." sign ahead!

9 PAST MODALS FOR OPINIONS AND ADVICE

A Read the sentences about what Sam and Bill did on the way to the wedding.
What should or could they have done instead? Use **should have** or **could have**
to express your opinion.

1) Bill drove his old car to the wedding.
He could have borrowed a newer car.

2) Sam and Bill stopped to buy something for the wedding on the way.

....

3) They didn't stay on Highway 41, so they weren't sure where they were.

....

4) Bill knew his gas gauge had been acting a little funny, but had done nothing about it.

....

5) Because of their problems, they weren't able to arrive an hour early for pictures.

....

6) Sam and Bill made Emily worry about what had happened to them.

....

B *Pair work* Take turns talking about what you would have done if these
things had happened to you. Use the modal **would have** in your responses.

1) You got lost on the way to your own wedding.

2) You arrived at your friend's wedding dressed too casually.

14 Behind the scenes in TV news

Preview

1 CULTURE

North Americans follow the news in a variety of ways. Many read a newspaper every morning, or listen to the news on their car radio on the way to work. Others read a weekly newsmagazine, check Internet sites, or watch the news on television in the evening. Typically, news programs are broadcast weekdays after work and late in the evening. Some cable news channels show news programs twenty-four hours a day.

How do people in your country follow the news? How is the news different on TV, in newspapers, on the radio, and in magazines? Which source do you prefer, and why? How often do you watch the news on TV?

2 VOCABULARY *Covering the news*

Choose phrases from the box to complete the sentences. Use the correct form of the verb.

✔choose a camera angle	deliver the news	shoot the pictures
cover the news	pick out a sound bite	write a script

1) A news photographer must ......*choose a camera angle*...... that will result in some interesting pictures.

2) For a television newscast, it's necessary to .... so that the person reading the news knows what to say.

3) Newscasters need to .... in an objective manner.

4) A news photographer .... that will be included in the nightly newscast.

5) I like the way Channel 4 .... It investigates stories thoroughly.

6) Sometimes a newscast can't show an entire interview, so they .... that summarizes an important point.

3 GUESS THE FACTS

What do you think these people who work at a TV news station do?

news anchor   reporter   assignment editor

 **Watch the video**

4 GET THE PICTURE

What are these people's jobs? Choose a job from the box and write it below each picture.

Alan Beck
associate news director

Keith Brown

Rod Wermager

anchor
assignment editor
✔associate news
  director
director
photographer
producer
reporter

Vince Irby

Carrie Hoerrmann

Leo Holmeister

Robyne Robinson

5 WATCH FOR DETAILS

A Complete the sentences with a job from Exercise 4.

1) The .... is in charge of daily operations.
2) The .... gathers story ideas and assigns the crew.
3) The .... conducts interviews.
4) The .... shoots the pictures.
5) The .... is the manager of the newscast.
6) The .... is the coordinator of the technical staff.
7) The .... delivers the news to the public.

B *Pair work* Take turns describing the people in part A like this:

The associate news director is the person who is in charge of daily operations.

55

Follow-up

6 WHAT'S NEWS?

A *Pair work* Imagine that you are assignment editors for a news station. Plan a thirty-minute local news program. Decide which stories from the list below to include, in which order they should appear in the newscast, and how many minutes you will spend on each story.

- Gladys Holt celebrates 100th birthday
- high school basketball team wins championship
- Mr. Martin's unusual garden
- mayor resigns
- weather forecast
- celebrity to visit local shopping mall
- new restaurant opens
- dog rescues boy from river
- school board to meet tomorrow
- President trips coming off plane

Evening Newscast

Stories	Minutes
•	☐
•	☐
•	☐
•	☐
•	☐
•	☐

B *Group work* Join another pair. Compare your news stories. Explain the reasons for your decisions.

7 ROLE PLAY *And here's the news!*

Pair work Imagine you work at a news station. One student is the anchor and the other is the reporter. Prepare a newscast item using one of the stories from Exercise 6 above. Practice your newscast, and then present it to the class.

Language close-up

8 WHAT DID THEY SAY?

Watch the video and complete the commentary. Then compare
with a partner.

The role of the anchors is explained.

Narrator: The anchors are the .... viewers see
.... the news. At this ....,
there are .... : a man and a woman. Robyne Robinson is
one of the ....

Robyne: .... anchor's job is .... But what
we usually do every day is we try to .... as much
as we can, ... to as much .... as we
can . . . uh . . . . as much .... on the other
.... and on the .... news
as possible. We take that .... , and we
write .... all day long with the help of
.... and .... and the
reporters and ....

Narrator: After the ...., Robyne and her ....
are the ones who .... the .... to the ....

---

9 PASSIVE *How a Web site is designed*

A Complete the sentences below about how a Web site is designed by using
the passive form of the verbs in parentheses.

.... A prototype .... (design) by the developers and .... (view)
by the client.

.... Approval .... (give) by the client to proceed with the project.

.... The Web site .... (test) and then .... (show) to the client for
final approval.

.... The finished Web site .... (put online) and may ....
(maintain) by the developer or the client.

...1... Ideas for the Web site .... (discuss) by the client and the Web developer,
and decisions about content have to .... (make).

.... The Web site .... (build) by the software team.

B *Pair work* Put the sentences above in order. Then take turns describing
how a Web site is designed. Use **first**, **next**, **then**, **after that**, and **finally**.

Entertainment or environment?
A town debates.

1 CULTURE

How are decisions made in towns in the United States? Many officials are elected by the residents of the town; others are appointed by these elected officials. Some laws are written by officials, and some laws are voted upon by residents. Town councils may hold open meetings, where anyone in the town can speak and give an opinion. Citizens with ideas or complaints often write letters to the officials or to the local newspaper.

How are decisions made in the community where you live? Have you ever been involved in a community decision? What do you think are some important issues facing your community now?

2 VOCABULARY *Describing locations*

A Which words in the box describe each location? Write the words under each picture. Words may be used more than once.

attractive	congested	dirty	entertaining	natural	noisy	polluted	serene

garbage dump

....
....

suburb

....
....

amphitheater

....
....

wildlife refuge

....
....

riverfront

....
....

downtown

....
....

B *Pair work* Compare your answers. Then think of additional words to describe each location.

3 GUESS THE FACTS

The town of Burnsville, Minnesota, is trying to decide whether to build an amphitheater. What do you think are two arguments *for* the amphitheater? What do you think are two arguments *against* it?

 **Watch the video**

4 GET THE PICTURE

Who is *for* the amphitheater? Who is *against* it? Check (✔) your answers.

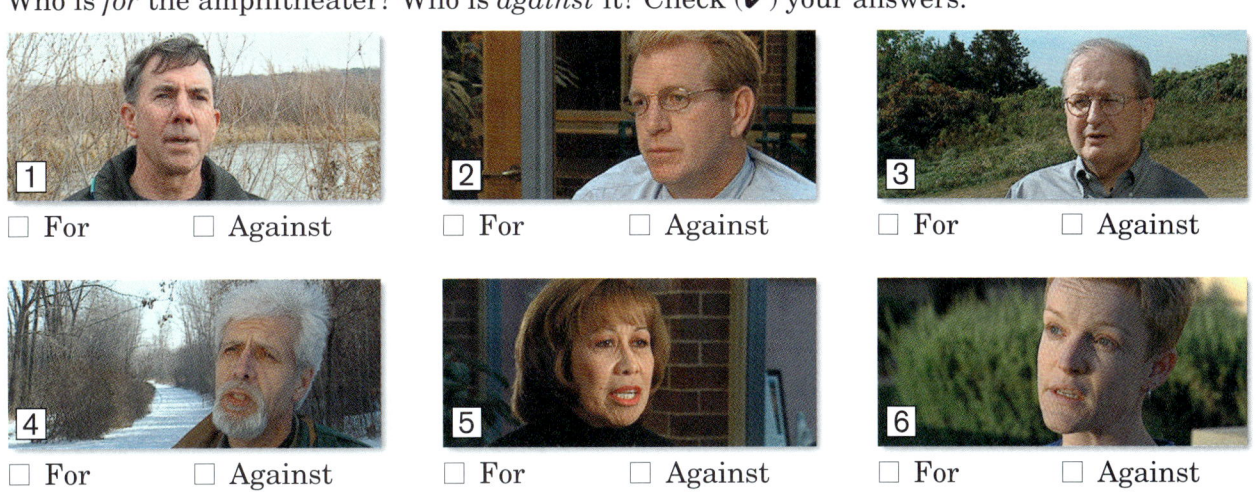

1 ☐ For ☐ Against	2 ☐ For ☐ Against	3 ☐ For ☐ Against
4 ☐ For ☐ Against	5 ☐ For ☐ Against	6 ☐ For ☐ Against

5 WHO SAID WHAT?

Who said the sentences below? Match each person from Exercise 4 with a sentence. Then compare with a partner.

.... "The amphitheater project . . . will allow us to . . . begin the cleanup of the riverfront so that our citizens can access the river."

.... "There isn't any indication that it's going to have a negative impact on the wildlife in the area."

....1.... "I'd prefer to see the area incorporated either into the National Wildlife Refuge System or be left as a natural area."

.... "So I think basically it's a . . . it's a bad plan and a bad idea."

.... "So if it means bringing in more revenue and obviously more culture to this area, then I'm all for it – definitely."

.... "In my opinion, it's going to create enormous problems with traffic."

6 GUESSING MEANING FROM CONTEXT

Read these sentences and guess the meanings of the underlined words.
Check (✔) your answers. Then compare with a partner.

1) It would provide a new source of revenue for the city. <u>On top of that</u>, the city would not have to finance an environmental cleanup of the former dump site.

☐ In addition   ☐ Nevertheless   ☐ However

2) It seems like a good idea, doesn't it? So what's the <u>controversy</u>?

☐ plan   ☐ cost   ☐ disagreement

3) The Minnesota Valley National Wildlife Refuge is a <u>sanctuary</u> for many species.

☐ proposal   ☐ disruption   ☐ safe place

4) The <u>impact</u> of nearly 20,000 people and thousands of vehicles will scare the wildlife out of the area.

☐ effect   ☐ fact   ☐ cause

5) The continuous noise of automobile traffic and the <u>sporadic</u> loud noises of occasional concerts shouldn't be compared.

☐ steady; constant   ☐ happening from time to time   ☐ entertaining

Follow-up

7 FOR OR AGAINST

A You are a resident of Pleasantville, a small town about fifty kilometers from a large city.
A recreation company has proposed building a golf course in Pleasantville in an area that is now a natural forest. Make a list of reasons *for* and *against* the golf course.

For	*Against*
would attract tourists	would endanger wildlife

B *Group work* Work in groups of four. Discuss the reasons *for* and *against* building the golf course. Then decide whether or not to build it. Use language like this:

In my opinion . . .	That's a good point. Nevertheless, . . .	On the other hand . . .
I feel that . . .	That's an interesting idea. However, . . .	I don't think that . . .

Language close-up

8 WHAT DID HE SAY?

Watch the video and complete the commentary. Then compare with a partner.

Reporter Adam Whisner explains the controversy surrounding the Burnsville Amphitheater.

Hi. I'm Adam Whisner, and I'm standing on the .... of the .... project, the Burnsville Amphitheater. Burnsville is a .... of Minneapolis, Minnesota, and it's .... on the .... of an important river that flows through the area. .... its supporters, the amphitheater is an .... to turn a little-used piece of land into an .... outdoor .... center. It would seat almost 20,000 people and .... a new source of .... for the city. On top of that, the city would not have to .... an environmental cleanup of the former .... That would be .... for by the .... It seems like a good idea, ... ? So what's the controversy?

9 PASSIVE MODALS *Talking about town rules*

TOWN RULES	
Cars are not allowed to park on the streets overnight.	People are not permitted to smoke in libraries.
Cell phones are banned in theaters.	Dogs are required to be on leashes at all times.
Children are not allowed to be outside after 10:00 P.M.	Homeowners are required to keep their lawns mowed and yards neat.

How do you feel about the town rules? Choose a modal from the box that shows how strongly you feel and rewrite each town rule.

ought to be	should be	has to be	mustn't be
shouldn't be	has got to be	must be	

1) *Cars should be allowed to park on the streets overnight.* ....

2) ....

3) ....

4) ....

5) ....

6) ....

61

16 The ultimate challenge

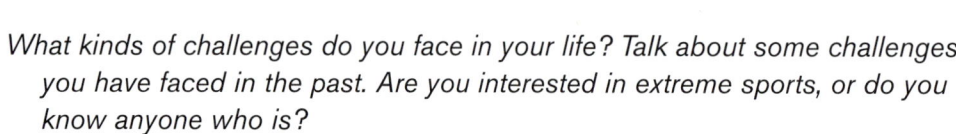
1 CULTURE

We need challenges to provide excitement and variety in our lives and to motivate us to succeed and to grow. People seek challenges and take risks in different ways. Some turn to extreme sports such as sky diving, mountain climbing, or white-water rafting. Other people satisfy their need for a challenge by excelling at their job, raising children, perfecting a skill, or learning a new language.

What kinds of challenges do you face in your life? Talk about some challenges you have faced in the past. Are you interested in extreme sports, or do you know anyone who is?

2 VOCABULARY *Synonyms*

A *Pair work* Put the words in the chart. Then add one more word to each list.

dream	gear	machines	morale	spirits	undertaking
fortitude	journey	✔mission	plan	supplies	vision

Goal	Expedition	Equipment	Mental strength
....	...mission...	....	....
....	....	....	....
....	....	....	....
....	....	....	....

B Discuss the following topics with a partner. Use words from the chart above.

1) Talk about one of your goals for the future.
2) Describe an expedition you've heard about or have been on yourself.
3) What kind of equipment do you need for a camping trip in the summer? in the winter?
4) What are some ways people can keep their mental strength in difficult situations?

3 GUESS THE FACTS

JAN 14 1993

What do you think these four women are planning to do? Check (✔) your answer.

☐ compete in a skiing competition

☐ camp in the winter for two months

☐ cross Antarctica on foot

Watch the video

4 GET THE PICTURE

Put the sentences in order (1 to 9).

.... A military supply plane dropped an unexpected package for the team.

.... Sunniva came down with a respiratory infection.

.... In Chile, bad weather delayed their departure for nine days.

.... The women decided to end their adventure with their arrival at the South Pole.

.... To keep on schedule, the team had to travel at least ten miles a day.

.... The four women were able to reach the South Pole.

.....*1*..... Ann's dream was to cross Antarctica without dogs, machines, or men.

.... Sunniva sprained her ankle.

.... Ann and her team were able to raise funds by asking schools for donations.

5 WATCH FOR DETAILS

A Write three pieces of information about each woman.

Ann Bancroft	Sue Giller	Anne Dal Vera	Sunniva Sorby
the expedition leader			

B *Pair work* Compare your information with a partner.

6 WHAT'S YOUR OPINION?

A Which of the following aspects of the Antarctic trip do you think would have been the most challenging for you? Rank them from 1 (most challenging) to 6 (least challenging).

.... raising money to finance the expedition

.... being in a small tent with the same person for four months

.... pulling a 110-kilogram sled uphill, against the wind

.... consuming 5,000 calories a day

.... traveling at least ten miles per day in freezing cold temperatures

.... having sore, cramped muscles

B *Pair work* Compare your ranking with a partner. Explain how you made your choices. Then talk about any other challenges that you think would have been difficult.

Follow-up

7 PLANNING AN EXPEDITION

A *Pair work* Imagine that you and your partner are going to be leaders of an expedition. Choose an expedition such as a trip down the Amazon River, a trek across the Sahara Desert, or an idea of your own. Complete the chart below as you plan your expedition.

Expedition:		
Necessary experience	*Equipment needs*	*Mental and physical challenges*

B *Group work* Get together with another pair or pairs. Take turns describing your expedition. Do any of the other students want to join your trip?

Language close-up

8 WHAT DID THEY SAY?

Watch the video and complete the commentaries. Then compare with
a partner.

The plan and preparation for the expedition is explained.

Narrator:	The .... was first to .... the 975 kilometers from the .... of Antarctica to the South Pole. This .... of the .... would be all .... and against the .... The .... 1,500 kilometers – from the South Pole to the .... coast – would be .... and .... the wind. The .... : to reach the .... side of the Antarctic .... in time to .... a free ride .... on a .... cruise ship.
Ann Bancroft:	So we .... the wheels .... , of becoming an .... , working on our .... and our ....
Narrator:	.... an enormous .... like this required .... of planning, ... , training, and ....

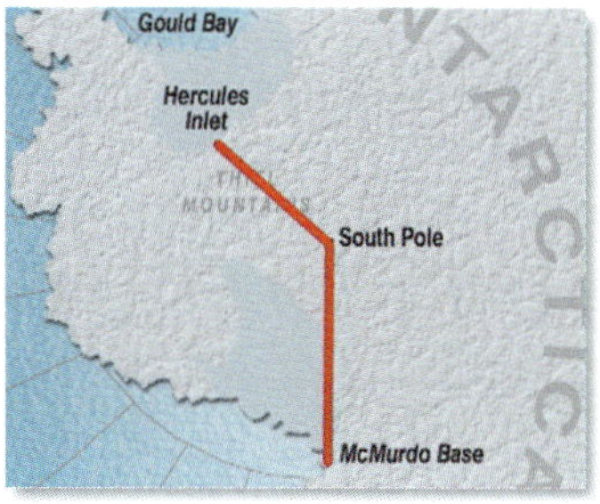

The map image shows:
- Gould Bay
- Hercules Inlet
- THE ... MOUNTAINS
- South Pole
- McMurdo Base
- ANTARCTICA

9 COMPLEX NOUN PHRASES WITH GERUNDS
Talking about challenges

A *Pair work* Tell a partner about a challenge you have faced in your life, such
as taking a trip, learning a new skill, or accomplishing a goal. Then choose five of the
questions below to ask about your partner's challenge. Write the responses below.

What was the most physically
challenging part?

What was the most mentally challenging part?

What was one of the rewards?

What was the most dangerous aspect?

What was the easiest part?

What was the most surprising
thing that happened?

What was the most exciting event?

What was the happiest moment?

What was the scariest moment?

What was the funniest moment?

1) *The most physically challenging part of Anita's canoe trip was paddling upstream against the wind.*

2) ....

3) ....

4) ....

5) ....

B *Group work* Join another pair. Explain your partner's challenge to them.

Acknowledgments

Illustrators

Keith Bendis 2, 18, 36

David Coulson 22

Felipe Galindo 12, 14 (*bottom*)

Daniel Vasconcellos 14 (*top*), 34, 35, 42, 45, 54

S.B. Whitehead 4, 5, 16, 17, 24, 40

Photographic Credits

2 (*top*) © Ariel Skelley/Corbis/Stock Market

6 (*top*) © Tony Savino/The Image Works; (*left to right*) © Jeff Dunn/Stock Boston; © Christies/Corbis; © Doris De Witt/Stone; © Raphaelle Peale/Francis G. Mayer/Corbis

8 (*bottom*) © Bernard Boutrit/Woodfin Camp/PictureQuest

9 (*top*) Francis B. Mayer/Corbis; (*bottom*) © Michael Newman/PhotoEdit

10 (*top*) © Roy Morsch/Corbis/Stock Market

22 courtesy Castle in the Country

26 (*top*) © David Young Wolff/Stone; (*left to right, top to bottom*) © VCG/FPG; © AP/Wide World; © David & Peter Turnley/Corbis; © Jim Steinberg/Photo Researchers; © Telegraph Colour Library/FPG; © Joel W. Rogers/Corbis

27 (*top*) © Frank Staub/Index Stock Imagery/PictureQuest

28 (*left to right, top to bottom*) © Gerry Ellis/Minden Pictures; © Daniel J. Cox/Stone; © John Guistina/FPG; © Stan Osolinski/Corbis/Stock Market; © Gerry Ellis/Minden Pictures

30 (*top*) © Lawrence Manning/Corbis; (*bottom*) © A. Ramey/PhotoEdit

32 (*left to right, top to bottom*) © Zigy Kaluzny/Stone; © B. Seitz/Photo Researchers; © James Marshall/Corbis; © Rick Gomez/Corbis/Stock Market

33 (*bottom*) © David Paul/The Image Bank

34 © eStock Photography/Photographer's Picture Library LTD/PictureQuest

38 (*top*) © Jeff Greenberg/PhotoEdit; (*left to right, top to bottom*) © Hulton-Deutsch Collection/Corbis; © Culver Pictures; © Bettmann/Corbis; © Bettmann/Corbis; © Brown Brothers; © /Hulton/Archive

41 (*bottom*) © Buddy Mays/Corbis

42 © Tom Tracy/Stone

46 © Catherine Karnow/Woodfin Camp

50 © Myrleen Ferguson/PhotoEdit/PictureQuest

54 © Bob Daemmrich/The Image Works

56 (*top*) © Tom Stewart/Corbis/Stock Market; (*middle*) © Steve Terrill/Corbis/Stock Market; (*bottom*) Journal Courier/The Image Works

58 (*top*) © Paula Lerner/Woodfin Camp; (*left to right, top to bottom*) © David R. Fraier/Photo Researchers; © Alan Schein/Corbis/Stock Market; © John Sohm/The Image Works; © Jim Brandenburg/Minden Pictures; © Victor Englebert/Victor Englebert; © Paul Harris/Stone

60 © David Madison/Stone

62 © Brian Bailey/Stone

64 © Peter Carmichael/Liaison Agency

Author's Acknowledgments

A great number of people assisted in the development of the *New Interchange* Videos. Particular thanks go to the following:

The **students** and **teachers** in the following schools and institutes who pilot-tested the Videos or the Video Activity Books; their valuable comments and suggestions helped shape the content of the entire program:

Athenée Français, Tokyo, Japan; **Centro Cultural Brasil-Estados Unidos**, Belém, Brazil; **Eurocentres**, Virginia, U.S.A.; **Fairmont State College**, West Virginia, U.S.A.; **Hakodate Daigaku**, Hokkaido, Japan; **Hirosaki Gakuin Daigaku**, Aomori, Japan; **Hiroshima Shudo Daigaku**, Hiroshima, Japan; **Hokkaido Daigaku, Institute of Language and Cultural Studies**, Hokkaido, Japan; **The Institute Meguro**, Tokyo, Japan; **Instituto Brasil-Estados Unidos**, Rio de Janeiro, Brazil; **Instituto Cultural de Idiomas**, Caxias do Sul, Brazil; **Instituto Cultural Peruano-Norteamericano**, Lima, Peru; **Musashino Joshi Daigaku**, Tokyo, Japan; **Nagasaki Gaigo Tanki Daigaku**, Nagasaki, Japan; **New Cida**, Tokyo, Japan;

Parco-ILC English School, Chiba, Japan; **Pegasus Language Services**, Tokyo, Japan; **Poole Gakuin Tanki Daigaku**, Hyogo, Japan; **Seinan Gakuin Daigaku**, Fukuoka, Japan; **Shukugawa Joshi Tanki Daigaku**, Hyogo, Japan; **Tokai Daigaku**, Kanagawa, Japan; **YMCA Business School**, Kanagawa, Japan; and **Yokohama YMCA**, Kanagawa, Japan.

The **editorial** and **production** team on *New Interchange* Video Level Three: Pam Bernstein, Sylvia P. Bloch, Patti Brecht, Karen Brock, Karen Davy, Hilary Grant, Pauline Ireland, Kathy Niemczyk, Bill Paulk, Mary Sandre, Howard Siegelman, and Mary Vaughn.

And Cambridge University Press **staff** and **advisors**: Kanako Aoki, Carlos Barbisan, Kathleen Corley, Kate Cory-Wright, Riitta da Costa, Peter Davison, Peter Donovan, Cecilia Gómez, Colin Hayes, Koen Van Landeghem, Alex Martínez, Nigel McQuitty, Carine Mitchell, Andy Paz, Dan Schulte, Catherine Shih, Alcione Tavares, Su-Wei Wong, and Ellen Zlotnick.

And a special thanks to the video producer, Master Communications Group.